URBAN AYURVEDA

Dr Tanya Malhotra completed her Bachelors of Ayurvedic Medicine and Surgery (BAMS) from Delhi University and, thereafter, did her post graduate study in Clinical Nutrition from Medvarsity. She first did her own research in Ayurveda and Vedanta Darshan (Vedic Philosophy) and, finally, from the age of 21 she began doing her bit for the community. In more than nine years of clinical practice, she has served as a House Physician for Government of NCT of Delhi and has been the youngest Nadi Physician for the Art of Living Foundation. She has represented Ayurveda in India and abroad, and was selected to represent Ayurveda in a leadership and management programme by the Indian School of Business and Goldman Sachs 10000 Women Entrepreneurs Certificate Programme.

Currently running two clinics in Delhi-NCR, she strives to make Ayurveda the preferred science of living for the youth of India. She can be reached at www.drtanyamalhotra.com.

URBAN AYURVEDA

Dr Tanya Malhotra

Published by
Rupa Publications India Pvt. Ltd 2017
7/16, Ansari Road, Daryaganj
New Delhi 110002

Sales centres:
Allahabad Bengaluru Chennai
Hyderabad Jaipur Kathmandu
Kolkata Mumbai

Copyright © Dr Tanya Malhotra 2017

The views and opinions expressed in this book are the author's own and the facts are as reported by him which have been verified to the extent possible, and the publishers are not in any way liable for the same.

All rights reserved.
No part of this publication may be reproduced, transmitted, or stored in a retrieval system, in any form or by any means, electronic, mechanical, photocopying, recording or otherwise, without the prior permission of the publisher.

ISBN: 978-81-291-4751-6

First impression 2017

10 9 8 7 6 5 4 3 2 1

Printed and bound in India by Repro Knowledgecast Limited, Thane

This book is sold subject to the condition that it shall not, by way of trade or otherwise, be lent, resold, hired out, or otherwise circulated, without the publisher's prior consent, in any form of binding or cover other than that in which it is published.

I dedicate this book to the divine within each of us who wishes to seek knowledge and health. For my daughter, Narayani, who came into my life while writing the book. In the loving memory of my father, Gopi Krishan Malhotra, who could foresee my future in Ayurveda

Contents

Introduction	ix
1. Know Thyself	1
2. Ayurveda for Everyday	17sswssw
3. Ayurveda for Every Season	35
4. Ayurveda for Work Life	50
5. Ayurveda for Students	65
6. Ayurvedic Cooking	74
7. The Way to a Healthy Life	98
Fall in Love with Yourself Again!	109
Acknowledgements	110

Introduction

We possess an inherent animalistic need to live in a herd; this herd, ages ago, firstly consisted of hunters and gatherers in the forests. The necessity of food made the hunters evolve into farmers, and the herds changed into villages, these villages became towns and towns have now become cities. In a way, we are back from where we came from. The previous jungle was Mother Nature's lap whereas the urban jungle has taken us away from nature; we are preoccupied with too much information and programming with no time to spend with ourselves. Success has become the first benchmark, and what we are continuously failing to understand is that being self-aware is the key to all things good in life because when one is established in oneself, only then can any worldly success become easy to attain.

    Once a pupil asked his guru, a sage, as to why people meditate? To which the sage smilingly replied that the ultimate quest of human life is knowledge. The penultimate book is one's own body and, therefore, if one seeks any answer, the solution lies in knowing your own self and that all the worldly desires can be fulfilled if one is firmly established in health or, in other words, one is firmly established in his/her own body. Indeed, as Aristotle also says, 'knowing yourself is the beginning of all wisdom'. The Vedic sciences, chiefly Ayurveda, has proved to be the most experienced science in the history of civilization and serves as a handy practical guide on all imaginable material and non-material aspects. It talks about life's worldly desires and spiritual aspects that go on simultaneously and one cannot be separated from the other. In each person the manifestation of these will be different. Ayurveda talks about the different kinds of profession and that it is important to earn money and equally important to realize about the self or the 'atman'.

Ayurveda literally translates to 'the science of life'. It is believed that this knowledge, essential for human life, was remembered, not just written, even before the development of human kind. This knowledge, coming naturally to us, is embedded in our subconscious mind. It is just that we have forgotten. Have you ever noticed that after so many years tradition is making a return and old is again becoming the new? We are again embracing our traditions. It is just that the traditional knowledge was always there, we were just misled for a while and now we are coming back on track because we have realized that this is indeed the healthier way of life. Even westerners have been known propagators and promoters of our Vedic sciences. I am here to connect the dots and provide the missing links so that your knowledge can again belong to you.

The fundamental binary principles

There are two main principles of Ayurveda, the first is to preserve the health of a healthy person and the second is to alleviate a patient from his/her disease. We do not just swear by the age-old saying, prevention is better than cure, we also swear by the mission, prevention and preservation of health because diseases are uncountable but health is only one. Ayurveda consists of a great deal of practical advice for every individual on almost every imaginable aspect of life. It also includes more specialized medical teachings on all aspects of diagnosis and therapy, aimed at the medical professional.

The triad of body, mind and spirit

The trinity concept of western methodologies has its root in the Vedic sciences. It is said that every living being has three faculties, the body, mind and spirit. The body is defined as *yat nitya sheerayate iti shariram* i.e. what decays every day is the body; death and disease are the two bitter truths of life. All of what we possess now, our body or our home, is temporary, as it is present for a few seconds, the next second it changes. Every second is a blessing. The body is in constant interaction with the external environment taking in or consuming what it requires and then flushing the unwanted part. I strongly feel that it is due to excessive consumerism that lifestyle disorders like obesity and diabetes have come up. Many people who have not yet developed any disease are, in fact, loaded with toxins and need to take rejuvenation therapies to restore themselves. We have only become consumers and have lost the art of moderation and methods of detoxification completely. We are going to understand how to detoxify and deconsumerize ourselves throughout the course of this book.

The mind is ever changing; it never stays at one place at one time. You might be physically present here but the mind has just come back from a return flight to Paris because you have always wanted to take yourself there. So, the mind is like the driver, it can drive you to paradise or to an accident. Technology is the material manifestation of the mind. It was somebody's mind only that thought that it wants to be connected with everybody all the time. Some of you must have experienced some connections with your guru or loved ones which cannot still be explained in technological terms and are beyond the conformities of a device. Of course we can switch off technology to be disconnected, but the important thing is to channelize this connection with the divine i.e. continuous energy of the universe; this way you will feel harmonious always. This will result in absolute focus, silent awareness and serene dynamism. Alas, the harmony is being strangled by stress these days.

Almost every patient in his first visit describes the mind as being stressed. Stress is defined as constant pressure exerted over anything or constant mental turbulence. I would, rather, describe stress as the feverishness of the mind. Fever, of course, is just a symptom of temperature rise in the body. However, Ayurveda describes fever as the continuous agony of the mind and body which may or may not result in rise of temperature that is *tapam*. Therefore, when it is said everyone is stressed what can be noted is that everyone is suffering from this agonizing burning of the mind. Mind becomes restless which, eventually, results in lack of focus and concentration further resulting in low efficiency. Mind is the sensory consumer of thoughts whereas body is the physical consumer of materials. In situations when you feel very low, immediately drink a glass of hot water to detoxify the body and take some time out for thoughtlessness for the mind. Sit and relax, and notice your breathing. Be in tune with your breath. If there are too many thoughts pouring in you may also go for guided or group meditation. In daily practices, too, one can adopt certain methodologies which are quite beneficial in the long run. Ayurveda says that silent awareness, courage, strong will, patience and pure knowledge are therapies of mind.

The soul on the contrary is not a consumer like the body or mind. It is just a spectator, a spectacular spectator at that. It is the pure, divine and unbounded energy of the cosmos. The union of the detoxified body and decosumerized mind with the divine is called *yoga*. All diseases really originate from the imbalance of the energy systems of the body, the constant flow of energy within the body and exchange of energy with the external environment results in optimization of the physical and even creative potential.

How do we understand what being healthy is?

Health, according to Ayurveda, is not merely an absence of disease or infirmity. It is the absolute balance of the physical, mental, physiological, social and spiritual aspects of life. The definition given by Sushruta states, 'Balanced *doshas* (body humours), healthy *agni* (digestive and metabolic fires), a synergistic state of *dhatus* (metabolic tissue) and *malas* (their metabolic end-products) lead to a balanced state of senses, mind and body which all lead to good health'. This concept was propounded at least thousands of years ago and is even more comprehensive than that given by WHO (World Health Organization) a few decades ago.

According to Maharishi Charaka, the abnormal state of body tissue and functional systems is called a disorder and their harmony is called natural health; happiness or *sukham* is the term used for health whereas misery or *dukham* is the term for any disease or disorder. The goal of life is true freedom from disease, enjoyment of uninterrupted physical, mental stability and contentment. For many, indulgence and fulfilment of all desires can only lead to contentment, this fancy notion of wishing for everything and getting to that is a mirage. Desires are never-ending fantasies of the mind. Ayurveda recognizes these desires and speaks in length about them.

Our uncountable desires vis-à-vis the three fundamental ones

To wish for a long life is one of three fundamental desires of human beings. The other two are the desire for money and for the divine. Desiring something is only human but when that want becomes a need, a need that you cannot do without, life becomes a constant struggle. If we focus purely on survival, life becomes miserable; if we focus on progress life becomes glorious. Just decide that health will be your priority and you have to be fit, everything else you desire shall follow. This is to be followed daily and requires discipline and dedication. However, I can make it easy for you. In this book we shall discuss about how to be healthy by adopting the simple Ayurvedic way. The technicalities of Ayurveda have been described in detail in tandem with the modern concept of wellness.

The three pillars of life

Ahara (food), *nidra* (sleep) and *abhramacharya/bhramacharya* (i.e. celibacy and non-celibacy at the required stages) are the pillars of life. Ayurveda is written in poetic verses in Sanskrit literature. It is very interesting to note that in this particular verse, there is *hrishva,* 'a' written just before bhramacharya. Bhramacharya literally means 'to act like the divine', to be pure and to be celibate. True celibacy will only be attained when the animalistic desire of copulation that crops up in various stages of life is somehow channelized. Ayurveda, being the most practical science, propagates the selective use of celibacy; it is to be followed with utmost diligence in the first quarter and the last quarter of life. Ayurveda prefers moderation as the golden mean. You will limit yourself or nature will limit you if you are just ignorant and indulgent. Yes, indulgence is a legitimate goal of life only when it is done at the right stage. There are four *purusharthas* of life i.e. goals: *dharma, artha, kama* and *moksha*.

Dharma, as is most widely misinterpreted, doesn't signify religion. It is, in fact, righteousness or discipline that is to be followed in the first stage of life, also throughout the life it is the goal of fulfilling the duties assigned to you. To define and fulfil your purpose not just for your family but for the whole society and mankind in a broader sense is dharma. So to attain knowledge as a student is dharma. Ayurveda is too pure a science to be confined in the boundary of one religion. For the physician, it guides him to treat anyone belonging to any region or way of life with same diligence. For the follower, it guides to seek the self which is a part of universal energy. Religion is not essential to life like food is. However, seeking or learning is like food for the mind which is quite essential.

Artha is the goal of accumulating possessions in the course of fulfilling your purpose; since we live in a material world, material possessions are a necessity. The key here, also, is moderation. Once we possess too many worldly possessions their safety and security again becomes a stress. Someone once said to me that he takes pride in giving rather than taking, I found him to be one of the most stable person I have known. The word *hridya* or heart in Sanskrit consists of three *aksharas:* '*hri*' means to take, '*da*' means to give and '*ya*' means to regularize or moderate it. It is our nature to take but to give is our actual purpose. We were dependents as babies, we again become dependents in old age, and to think that we are independent in the youth is a common anomaly we all make. Give when you can because you are taking in since the day you were born.

Kama is the goal of satisfying legitimate desires with the help of one's own accumulated possessions. If desires are left unattended and unfulfilled it creates a huge gap in the satisfaction quotient of the mind, but desires should be legitimate and should not harm anyone. Your freedom ends where the other person's freedom begins.

Moksha is the goal of realizing that there is more to life, than dharma, kama and artha. It is means to the breakage of all bindings, desires with absolute stillness.

Maharshi Vagbhatta once said that every man who needs to achieve all four goals i.e. dharma, artha, kama and moksha, needs to follow the direction of Ayurveda with utmost diligence. He added that to pursue and fulfil any aim, you will need a healthy body throughout. Otherwise most of the time will go in curative measures. Body is the temple of mind and all diseases crop up because of the lack of love towards one's own self. I have specially seen this phenomenon in the urban working mothers who have so much love and care for their family and work but when it comes to their own body they are careless and sometimes, even clueless. Careless because they are multitasking the whole time and clueless because whatever time they get for themselves is spent in trying to follow 'fitness fads' or the passing health tips that fill the newspaper. Nowadays food patterns of urban homes are changing from Indian to continental style of cooking with more of salads, one of the frequent ingredient of salads is bell pepper. The bad news is that it doesn't suit everybody, especially if it is raw or if there is increased heat element in the body. The solution is to always try to either steam or sauté bell peppers. The same applies to carrots, lettuce, etc. to just make them easier to digest.

I would like to emphasize here that food acts as fuel for the body, it should increase the output and efficiency and not decrease it, so if there is feeling of dullness, restlessness or lack of focus after eating it means that whatever you ate was not suitable for your body or the quantity was a bit too much to handle for the body. It is the continuous over stuffing of the body over so many years that diseases crop up. If you join the palms of your hands so it can hold water in it, that unit of volume is called *Anjali* in Ayurveda which is unique to each individual. Anjali is the amount one should eat in one go, yes, this varies from person to person that is why the exact measurement can't be standardized. The standard formula given by Ayurveda is to divide our stomach into four equal parts—two parts should be filled with solids, one part should be filled with liquids and one part should be left for the proper movement of the food. Our intestines need at least this much space for the proper churning, absorption and propulsion of food. If these rules are not followed, disorders of digestion like constipation, acidity and indigestion are bound to arise. At this point I would like to mention a golden rule: that it is always better to eat less than to eat more. Have you ever noticed that the number of people dying of overeating has always been more than people dying of hunger? Delhi has emerged, in the last decade, with the dubious honour of being the diabetes capital of the world. A title we should be ashamed of considering how many people sleep hungry in India. Surely, as it is said, Mother Earth has enough for everyone's need but not enough for everyone's greed.

Now, when I say this, my patients ask me that how is it possible that there are a lot of people who eat anything and everything and still manage to remain healthy, yet when they make the smallest of mistake they tend to feel heavy, bloated and can even fall sick?

Chapter One

Know Thyself

The answer to the question in the introduction lies in knowing your *prakriti* (constitution) and then getting to know about your *agni* (digestive and metabolic fire). Prakriti and agni both are very unique and accurate concepts of Ayurveda which help you to decide in which realm you fall into. A person of *pitta* prakriti might think that he/she can digest everything and can get away with a bit of overeating also, this overeating will make that person severely prone to allergies, especially of the skin and digestive tract. Over a period of time they are also prone to develop high-cholesterol disorders and other cardiovascular diseases because the overeating tends to pollute their blood. It might not show during the youth but proves to be quite troublesome in later years.

So, to help you in knowing your prakriti I have compiled a set of Q&A which shall make you aware of your psycho-physiological nature i.e. prakriti.

Please note that the following questionnaire is a ready reckoner for your personal use which will help you to know your physiology better and I suggest that the use of this should not be extended to others, as that is best left to an Ayurvedic practitioner.

Each question has three options, whichever you find closest to your personality give that one point. Also, in some questions you find two options equally suitable in your case so give one point each in that scenario.

Your answers don't have to be right or wrong, they just have to be the option which is the most appropriate for you; it is not that you will fall under only one category. Your points will be a mixed bag of all three columns as the human body is composed of all three humours i.e. vata, pitta and kapha which give rise to type v, type p and type k respectively. We will discuss in length about problems and solutions in detail, before that one needs to understand the nature of these elements in the body. Therefore, it is imperative to understand the nature of vata, pitta and kapha to understand how a prakriti is established in an individual. (Table is on the facing page.)

Understanding the universe within us

'*Yatha pinde tatha bhramanda*', (micro cosmos is the miniature of the macro cosmos) meaning 'as is the universe so is the body'. The human body is like a replica of the universe itself. This quote has been the basis of Vedic understanding since time immemorial. In the 20th century, we used to think that we were quite different from other species on the planet, but recent studies have proven that, in fact, the genetic code of a moss is very similar to that of a human. Therefore, as we define the universe and its entire species in a more intricate manner we will soon come to realize that the basis of human species is, in fact, the replica of the universe itself. '*Pinda*' refers here to the body, and '*bhramanda*' has been interpreted both as Earth in micro view and the universe in macro view. The only discrepancy here is that the universe is continuous (or, rather, seems continuous) because it has more gazillion life

KNOW THYSELF ♦ 3

Criteria	Type K	Points	Type P	Points	Type V	Points
Physical built	Stout with strong built, round and broad shoulders, well-developed physique		Medium with moderate built		Thin with prominent bones, flat and small shoulders	
Complexion	Even complexion, sometimes tending towards pale		Red, ruddy, flushed, pinkish complexion		Dullness, specially dark patches	
Skin texture	Thick, smooth, moist, cold, soft		Warm, moist, pink, tends to develop acne, moles and freckles		Thin, dry, rough, cracked, prominent veins, develops early wrinkles	
Hair texture	Thick, wavy, soft but sometimes oily, lustrous in finish		Soft, silky, straight, moderate in texture, tends to have grey hair and hair fall early in life		Rough and coarse to touch, thin in texture, dull finish, wavy	
Eyes and brows	Prominent, white, attractive eyes, with thick eyelashes and brows which grow easily		Bright piercing eyes with thin eyelashes and brows, get red easily		Small, dry eyes with thin eyelashes and brows tending towards dull, get dry easily	
Digestion	Moderate, solid and soft stool, may have mucous secretions		Good, tending towards diarrhoea, prone to acidity		Variable, tending towards constipation, prone to bloating, dry, hard stool	
Appetite	Constant appetite but low, can't eat big portions		Strong and sometimes uncontrollable appetite		Variable, sometimes depends on emotions	
Sleep pattern	Deep sleepers, tend to fall sleep easily		Moderate, wakes up easily, tend to fall asleep again		Superficial, sometimes tending towards insomnia	

Criteria	Type K	Points	Type P	Points	Type V	Points
Body odour	Moderate sweating with pleasant smell		Profuse sweating with strong odour		Scanty, no odour	
Immunity	Good, consistent, has high endurance power		Medium, prone to allergies and infections		Prone to diseases, has seasonal illnesses	
Disease resistance	Obesity, tendency to gain weight, water retention		Cholesterol disorders, prone to infections, fever and skin infections		Pain, arthritis, nervous system disorders	
Sensitivity	Sensitive to extreme cold climate, dampness and high moisture makes them dull		Sensitive to extreme hot climate, winters are more suitable		Sensitive to extreme cold and extreme hot climate, tends to develop dryness	
Voice texture and speech pattern	Slow and definite in talking, smooth and pleasant voice texture, good pitch		Argumentative and convincing, moderate voice texture, high pitch, sharp tone		Quick to start, talkative but inconsistent, hoarse voice, weak and erratic	
Temperament and memory	Slow and calm to take notice, don't forget things, sentimental and attached		Confident, sharp and clear memory, tend to get angry and irritable easily		Anxious, nervous, notice things easily, tend to forget, fearful and insecure	
Dream pattern, if any	Dream of romance but seldom has dreams		Few dreams but of colourful, passionate, conflicting nature		Many dreams of flying and moving, restlessness in dreams	
Sexual nature	Constant desire, delayed expression		Passionate but dominating		Variable, erratic, deviant	
Physical movement	Slow-paced walkers, lethargic to start movement		Motivated, firm-footed walkers		Quick, erratic, hyperactive, fast walkers	

years than we do, and our body on the other hand has a timeline. So, if we have to increase our lifespan or improve the quality of our health, we simply have to follow the rules formed by nature itself, our universe is the biggest teacher. If we are diligent enough to notice that it is a self-sustaining system that has enough changes in itself to maintain the continuum of life.

Just like there is wind in the universe, there is vata in our body providing movement and speed; just like there is sun in the universe, our body has pitta and just as there are rivers and mountains in the universe similarly there is kapha element in the body. The macro cosmos is quite similar to the micro cosmos. The five basic elements (earth, water, fire, air and space) combine to form the three following humours in the physical body on which our lives and prakriti are based.

The three humours

Vata, pitta and kapha are the three humours of the body. These form, maintain and vitiate the body. Even at the time of birth their combination results in the formation of our prakriti or constitution. It is the reason of diseases or good health running in a particular family. The humours along with the tissue system and the malas (waste) make up the body at any given point of time. *Dosh-dhatu-mal-moolam-hi-sharirram* i.e. your body is constantly working, maintaining, creating waste and eliminating at the same time. It is a very intelligent and marvellous machine. And these three *doshas* (humours) are the basis of that mechanism.

Humour	Vata	Pitta	Kapha
Mahabhootas	aakash+vayu	agni	prithvi+jala
Element	quintessence (sky)+air	fire	earth+water

VATA

Vata comes from the phrase *va gati gandhanayo* means 'that which provides gati or speed is vata'. It provides movement that is minute, as well as big. The essential rhythms of the body like breathing, heartbeat and the physical movements like walking, writing, etc. are all provided by healthy state of vata energy.

Even movement of mind, which is thinking, is governed by vata. *Utsah* meaning positive thinking or enthusiasm is the natural tendency of state of balanced vayu. Blinking, nerve impulses, expulsion of waste from the body are all the other innumerable examples of essential movements of the body. These are all governed by vata. It is the carrier of the other two humours (pitta and kapha) and holds a primary importance in both natural and unnatural manifestation of health.

Site: It dwells in the whole body; however, its primary seats are the colon (large intestine), hips, thighs, ears, bones and the skin. Out of all these also the primary seat is identified as the colon.

Function: Even high physical energy is also due to equilibrium of vayu in the body and tiredness shows vitiation. Similarly, if one tends to overthink, it is like overusing a natural mechanism and if the thoughts are not in the right direction, it leads to negativity. This is how I define stress. This creates a vicious circle. Stress further tends to aggravate vata dosha, first in the mind then in the body. Stress is that restlessness (vata) which needs to be constantly eliminated from the body; if it becomes constant with no outlet for a long period of time it takes the form of a disease be it in the mind or the body. This was taken in account as the major cause of disease only recently. On the other hand, vayu is main the precursor of any permanent disease in the body according to Ayurveda. The rest of the humours, both pitta and kapha, are rendered handicapped. Such is the importance and power of the vata dosha.

Vitiation: Hypoactivity, that is lack of movement, and hyperactivity are the causative factors for vitiation and are all signifiers of underlying vata disorder. Like the air in the environment which can be only felt and known by properties, vata is also known by its physical attributes in the body, the gunas like ruksha (dry), sheeta (cold), laghu (light), khara (rough), chala (mobile), sukshma (subtle) and rarefied. The hypersensitivity to extreme climates, like intolerance to extreme winters and extreme summer is also a signifier of increased state of vitiated vata disorder. One may have a strong craving for warm food and beverage constantly when vayu is particularly aggravated in the colon. Constipation, lack of energy, loss of sleep, fatigue, emaciation, abdominal distension (rounded belly) are all physical symptoms of vitiated vata. These may not be taken as any particular illness but may lead to aggravated disease-causing mechanisms if vitiated vayu is not tapped at any early stage. Similarly, fear, anxiety, insecurity, confusion and irrelevant talking are signifiers of the aggravation of the mental faculty of vata and may result in psychological disorders if not curbed at the right time.

Prakriti analysis: Type V

If you have given maximum points to the column Type V in the prakriti table then your prakriti is that of a vata-predominant individual. People high on creative energies, always on the go, find it extremely tough to stay in one place patiently, they have an unpredictable appetite; sometimes high, sometimes low which is difficult to ascertain, making them the most prone to diseases and hence require an extremely disciplined lifestyle regimen. They should avoid foods that are dry in nature/served cold/extra hot beverages and keep a check on intake of excessive proteins, exercises like yoga and pilates works best for them as it require more stretching and relaxing. Sesame seed oil is the best remedy for vatas, they should apply it locally, consume it internally through nasya and eating. Food should be taken as per the hunger; avoid both overeating and fasting. Include a sufficient quantity of oils and fats in your diet as your body tends to dry up very fast. Linseed and olive oil is also good for you. Cleansing fruits like papaya, guava, pear, pomegranate and prune are excellent snack options. If the second highest points have gone to Type V means either the sub-dosha is vata that means you have a mixed prakriti or there is aggravation of vayu in the body.

Reason for aggravation of vayu are many and find increasing space in our lives with the advent of modern lifestyle, inadequate sleep, erratic schedules, being awake at night, not eating at regular time, eating while not hungry, too much work, physical and mental strain to the body, all tend to aggravate vayu. Bio-purification through herbs and oils is needed to curb this vayu. A simple solution would be to strictly follow daily and seasonal regimen, and this aggravation will automatically reduce from the body with consequent passage of time.

PITTA

Pitta is formed by the opposing elements of fire and water. This makes it very interesting as not only is it the faculty of the basic fire and energy system of the body; it is also the only dosha of transformation. It is pitta only which governs what changes into what, like solid food changes into liquid and then soluble nutrients. Pitta is responsible for the mental attributes like focus, discrimination and processing of thoughts. On the other hand, reception of sensory and motor data is the karma of vayu.

Site: It sits in mainly the small intestine, and also in stomach, sweat, sebum (oil secreting glands of the skin) and in the eyes. It is responsible for digestion, metabolism and absorption of food, maintenance of the temperature of the body, visual perception, lustre of skin, urge of hunger and thirst, intelligence, determination, courage and softness of the body.

Pitta may be aggravated due to increased intake of substances that are hot in potency like salty, oily, spicy food, consumption of alcohol, smoking, unsatisfied hunger for a continuous period of time or hot climatic conditions.

Function: The molten lava of the volcanoes is very rich in minerals but cannot be utilized until it cools down to a certain temperature, when it combines with the soil it leads to the growth of rich flora and fauna. One might understand the nature of pitta through this example. Pitta in its natural, unaffected stage, meaning at bodily temperature, adds the gunas of heat, light, fluidity, subtleness, sharpness, softness, clarity and aroma to our body, which makes a great foundation for the growth and upkeep of the body, but if it gets aggravated it consumes our own body just like a fire consumes a forest. It, again like the other two faculties, dwells in the whole body, albeit it forms the main constituent of the blood and plasmatic systems of our body.

Vitiation: It causes a variety of symptoms upon aggravation which are marked by desire for cold food, cold drinks, cool clothing and cooler environment. Aerated drinks, if taken at this stage, aggravate this fire in the body which is quite the opposite of what the popular belief is; because of the high carbonate and acid content they end up destroying the body more. Same is with ice or icy cold water. It is very easy to notice that ice can burn your skin leaving a rash if held for a long time, so in Ayurveda because of this latent energy of the ice, it is considered to be *ushna veerya* or the ultimate effect of ice on the body is that of increasing pitta. So, eating or drinking out of the refrigerator may harm you more than you realize. Let it rest outside for a while till it reaches the normal temperature. If one can reduce the habit of consuming refrigerated water down to minimum, you may see how your body is detoxifying itself in less than two weeks. By cool drinks here, it is advised to take khus sherbet, rose sherbet, water cooled in an earthen pot, bael juice, coconut water, basically liquids which are cool by their own nature. These are excellent hydrants for the ever-sweating pitta body.

Prakriti analysis: Type P

Digestion and metabolism are very sensitive areas of the pitta prakriti person. General symptoms of excessive thirst, excessive hunger, burning sensation in the skin, body, eyes or hands are caused by pitta aggravation. It may also lead to hypersensitivity of the skin, prone to allergic reaction, rashes, boils, zits, pimples, etc. if symptoms are not subsided by taking a therapeutic diet they may further accentuate to fever, giddiness, diarrhoea, yellow discolouration of eyes, skin, stool, etc. which relates to the occurrence of an infection/inflammation in the body.

The mental attributes of pitta pertains to perfectionism and attention to detail, when this is not achieved, which is the case at times, may lead to anger, aggression, irritability. Pitta prakriti people tend to be more competitive, jealous, ambitious and short-tempered than other counterparts.

If you have scored most in Type P, you belong to the pitta prakriti group. Many of you will tend to have it as second scoring or subdosha in duo dosha prakriti. Pittas are the tigers of the pack, brave, intelligent, egoist, with a strong piercing gaze and radiant skin; they are easiest to notice in a group. However, on the flip side, they sweat a lot, have tendency to develop more freckles/moles/zits on their faces, ruddy complexion, moderate physical strength, less tolerance to hunger and thirst, craving for sweets and the first ones to react and sometimes get angry at a given situation. Please take care of your hair if you have scored most in the pitta column, hair tends to fall or turn white very early in life.

Pittas should limit the intake of both salt and spices as there is already excess heat in the body; also, extremely sour substances like vinegars which are acids and may prove very bad for your health. Drink water at room temperature in the morning, water in silver vessel or earthen pot is extremely good for you on an empty stomach. As a rule, have sweet-based breakfast in the morning, if you avoid spice, sour and caffeine in the morning, it will become a cakewalk to maintain your health. For diabetics, one may opt for fruit-based breakfast or sugar-free cereal meal. Make lunch your principle meal of the day. Avoid alcohol and their kind (substances containing alcohol) as your body gets way more damaged than the others. Since you can digest sugar in moderation, fruits like melons, dates, grapes, coconut, figs are good for you. Coriander, cumin, fennel seeds are great spices to be included regularly in the diet. Black pepper should be preferred as a dressing. Vegetable juices are extremely good detoxifiers for excessive heat in the body. Ghee or, as the westerners call it, clarified butter, is one substance you should have in moderation as it pacifies the hunger of the pitta person. In fact, if you have ghee as a regular, moderate garnish over you rice, roti and lentils, you will tend to feel more satisfied and full with lesser than the usual quantity. Coconut and olive oil are also good for you; stay away from refined oils as with the recent use of refined oils in our diet it is seen that pittas tend to develop more disorders of the cardiovascular system like high blood pressure, cholesterol imbalances, etc.

KAPHA

The combination of water and earth elements results in kapha dosha in the body. By this term we do not mean phlegm or just mucous of the body. These mucosal secretions in the noses, sinuses, throat and lungs originate from the kapha dosha but not kapha itself. Kapha is like the strong base on which the building of body is built. It is the stabilizer of the body and is responsible for maintaining the softness, moisture and lubrication of the body.

Site: It forms the shape and stamina of the body and flows/dwells in the whole body. However, the main site has been identified as the stomach where it accumulates on aggravation and causes diseases. The other major sites are in the chest, throat, heart, pancreas, ribs, stomach, plasma, fat tissue, nose and tongue.

Function: The main functions of kapha are support, sustenance, maintenance, healing and it is one of the major factors of immune-modulation. The physical attributes of kapha are cold, wet, heavy, slow, dull, static, smooth, dense and cloudy.

Vitiation: Lack of exercise, sitting for a long time, excessive sleeping and sleeping in the day, overeating, eating more carbohydrates and fats, excessive sugar in the diet, all aggravate the kapha dosha.

When kapha gets aggravated, there is loss of appetite, nausea, vomiting, heaviness in the body, pallor of skin, cold hands and feet, swollen joints, cough with phlegm, excessive sleep, lethargy and lack of concentration. One should have bitter, astringent and pungent tasting items of hot potency. All spices are examples of this, especially big cardamom, black pepper, etc.

Prakriti analysis: Type K

Imagine a white swan swimming through a lake looking graceful, patient, serene and well-paced with a peaceful gaze, that is how one can describe a person of kapha prakriti. If you have scored most in Type K you belong to the kapha group. Many of you will have a combination of pitta-kapha or vice versa as it tends to be common in Indians. In that case one needs to follow a bit of both the regimens according to the score-percentage.

Kapha prakriti people are reflections of the physical attributes of water and earth elements in the body. They are opposite in character to vata people. Kaphas are large in body frame and tend to weigh more than others. Despite of the outer stout frame they are rather delicate and emotional, they have thick, oily, cool skin with a pale complexion. Their bones are firm and joints are well rounded and well covered with muscles and fat. Eyes are big, attractive with thick eyelashes. Teeth are strong, white, well formed. Appetite and thirst are both slow but regular and steady. They tend to feel less thirsty than others so it becomes very important to develop a habit of drinking at least a glass of water stored overnight in a copper vessel, as it provides the necessary energy in the morning. They are the ones who abstain from hard physical work, although they have the actual capacity to do it steadily. They are intelligent, patient, stable minded, friendly and have a clear, melodious and sonorous voice. If they set their mind out to achieve something they can do so easily, otherwise they tend to be lazy and lethargic. Kaphas should strictly adhere to the rule of moderate eating, as one is blessed with a strong body, one needs to listen to the inner rhythms of the body and eat only when appetite is strong; kaphas should strictly avoid sleeping after eating and should go for a regulated fast once a week, they should not eat in large quantity or fatty foods e.g. cheese, butter, etc. They should include spices in the diet, especially black pepper, big cardamom, amla, harar, cumin, ajwain, ginger, curcumin, etc. Hot water is an excellent medicine for kaphas to reduce the cold and dampness in the body. They tend to tolerate summers better than winters. They should be cautious with food and regular with exercise so as to maintain their weight.

Hence it is imperative to understand the difference between dosha and prakriti. All of us have vata, pitta and kapha. But because of the predominance of one of these three and the difference in the qualitative attributes, we tend to have different likes and dislikes, tolerance, appetite and even tendency to have diseases. So the kapha dosha is present in all of us.

Combination prakriti

If you have scored almost equally in all the three columns, it can be ascertained that the body is maintaining a healthy state of equilibrium among the three faculties of the body and hence just the seasonal regimen needs to be followed and it will prevent most of the diseases, and promote the immaculate capacity of self-healing of the body. This is called *samdosha prakriti*, it is considered the healthiest of the lot.

There will be many of you who will score in not one but two columns, then a quantitative assessment has to be made and accordingly both the regimens have to be followed in that specific percentage.

It is very difficult to treat a pitta prakriti person with a disease of pitta origin; similarly, kapha prakriti with a kapha disease and so on and so forth. Means that whatever is already in predominance in your body needs to be managed with even more diligence and care because it tends to increase all the more easily. Therefore, to understand oneself and to let it heal on its own naturally is the purpose of this exercise. One is meant to enjoy certain things and abstain from others, it may not be the same case which each one of us. This disengagement in our own prakriti (nature) leads to comparison which in turn leads to conflict of the mind. The age-old proverb of how all our fingers differ in length stands true almost every time. It is very interesting to see how much our human body can teach us.

This prakriti is decided at the time of our conception and is nurtured through gestation. So, just as one tends to inherit a certain facial structure or feature from our parents, we also inherit these qualitative variations of doshas in the body. The fact that it is nurtured throughout gestation and has variation with the change of age, we contribute towards building our own prakriti and, of course, personality.

Different stages of life correspond to different stages of doshas

It is fascinating how children are unfailingly happy all the time, Ayurveda says that by virtue of age, kapha is predominant in childhood, pitta gains supremacy in youth and as we age vata reigns supreme and results in the natural emaciation of the body. By this very wonderful concept it can be understood that intelligence, patience and stable mindedness, which are natural attributes of kapha, tend to decrease as we grow up, and aggression, determination, anger tend to increase in the youth which then results in fear, anxiety, impatience and intolerance in old age. To counteract this natural *maya*, spend as much time with kids, they will never refrain from teaching you without making even the slightest of effort.

Ayurveda is without a beginning and without an end; it is continuous because of its timeless concepts. Hence it is apt to call it universal, as it applies to all life. Also, taking just the subject of the human body which is in constant interaction with the universe, it is quite evident that changes in the external environment lead to corresponding changes occurring with the health systems of the body. Let's take for example the recent climatic changes, it is easy to notice that with the increase in pollution and consequent global warming the carbon content of air has increased. Therefore, more and more people suffer from disorders of movement (vata disorders) and diseases of the thermogenic systems of the body (pitta).

The solution lies in being adaptive to change; change is the only constant rule of the universe. If humans have made negative changes on the Earth, the diseases have increased correspondingly. Sustainable development with environmental care can actually lead to decrease in the healthcare expense of any country. We, as a species, have failed to recognize this simple fact and have tried to change the nature according to our convenience resulting in climatic changes, which in turn has backfired even in the health trends. The quantitative life both in terms of number of living humans and the increase in the lifespan has been achieved, by studying the medical trend; the qualitative disorders of health have also simultaneously increased. We are more diseased and suffering more than the previous generation. A basic knowledge of the natural law stated in the Vedas can really help us balance this; the purpose is to amalgamate the best of all sciences to achieve the best in one's self.

Whole Earth is my home;
I thank the air for letting me breathe,
I thank water for nourishing me, Earth for providing for me,
I thank thee; let my mind be in knowledge,
Knowledge is the only reason to be!

Chapter Two

Ayurveda for Everyday

It is famously said, 'What cannot be achieved in a day'. All great things in life do happen only on a single day. It might take months or years of preparation for the actual event, yet it comes down to just a few hours of pure performance. To make the most of every single moment of life, one has to be at the healthiest best. As an event or presentation takes time to prepare so does your body. Have you noticed that in the excitement of the preceding big event in life, we tend to fall sick pretty often, for example, one might catch fever just before an important office meeting? Yes, we all blame stress, but on the contrary it is the haphazard routine that precedes the task. Reducing sleeping hours, increasing intake of coffee and other caffeinated drinks, eating at odd timings, basically compromising on health makes us fall sick. To avoid falling sick don't avoid the meeting, change the haphazard schedule and maintain a regular one.

It is always great to follow the example of children who also tend to fall sick during examination, therefore I advise them to study in the same time period as the examinations allotted time so that the brain is simultaneously programmed to be the most active during that three-hour period. Similarly, if you are preparing for an important meeting make yourself more active especially during that time of the day.

On the contrary, it takes only a few minutes of any incident to waste your whole day or to make your whole day. A bad meal might act as a hindrance to the focus or energy levels, the current Indian diet, which is very different from a vitalizing Vedic diet, contains a lot of *bhoona masala* which increases the sugar craving. The wholesome Indian meal drains you of energy as it brings all of the agni (heat element) to the center of the body. The suggestion here is to have something uncooked like salad or fruit at least once a day to balance out the heat of the overly cooked food. Also in the consequent chapters we will be discussing Vedic cooking which in fact tones down on spice and tones up on simple, fresh and efficient ways of cooking.

It has been noticed that reduction in energy levels is seen in older people, it is true for most people that same energy levels cannot be expected in the '50s as they were in your '20s, however in these cases exceptions are always there. You can achieve gradual increase in the energy of the body by following Vedic-day regime, once you start making these little changes, within a few days, there will be increase in focus, energy, memory and other functions of the body comparable to the most efficient people in your age group.

Everyday regimen

An *'ahoratra'* is the word used to describe 24 hours in Ayurveda, which like all Vedic sciences, provides a very scientific division of time. *'Dinacharya'* or daily schedule is the part which provides a beautifully described regular, disciplined, detailed regimen of the day for the optimal utilization of an amazing work resource of abundant energy i.e. the human body. This dinacharya encompasses methods of the minute detoxification, rejuvenation of every single part of the body, all that can be done during the day very easily to reduce ageing, maintaining energy levels, skin care, etc. on a daily basis.

Waking up

- Ayurveda advises that the ideal time to wake up is Bhramamuhurutam i.e. two hours before sunrise; it is the most peaceful time in the morning when nature itself awakens to welcome the Sun, our ultimate source of life and energy. Interestingly, research suggests that it is time when the fewest robberies take place as it is the least time of any kind of stress making it the best time to meditate, study or research.
- This is an ideal case scenario. You can adapt it in the present setting by waking up with school-going kids i.e. between 6 a.m. to 7 a.m. For those who already have kids, schedule your morning in such a way that you have time for self-preparation for a busy day ahead. The point here is to have an ideal time gap between waking up and going to office to cleanse and then nourish the body.
- Splashing of water on face should be done first thing after waking up, followed by rinsing of mouth, and splashing water on the eyes, this is a very effective exercise for the eyes. All this has to be done with regular, room temperature water.
- Proper voiding of bowel is quite essential and allot a specific time for this because if you feel that there is no natural urge for defecation, you may need to sleep a bit more. However, if you feel proper passing of stool doesn't take place on its own, taking triphala a night before will help in regularization of the schedule. It is an effective detoxifier and it is not habit-forming in most cases. Most of the other laxatives available in the market

are habit-forming and in case of regular usage end up drying the intestinal lumen, resulting in loss of essential electrolytes. Fruits like papaya, watermelon, pomegranate, sweet lemon (mausambi) and beetroot are excellent gastro cleansers and should be included in the diet in case of habitual constipation.

- Cleansing the bowel first thing in the morning is mandatory for the release of toxins and to have a light feeling. The position of squatting is very useful to relax the involuntary sphincter of the anus; one can use a small stool with the western toilet to improve the sitting posture on the toilet seat so as to relax the evacuating area of the lower body completely. Indians, in general, abide by this direction, however, due to lack of proper toilet-training skills in children nowadays it has been noticed that school-going children are developing unhealthy habits of cleansing the bowel in the afternoon. This creates a lot of tamasic or negative energy in the body. Also, if your stool is not well-formed that is it is greasy, watery, discoloured or spilt, it may signify an inflammation of the digestive tract. Medical (Ayurvedic) consultation should be done in these cases as there a lot of patients with chronic or latent gastrointestinal infections who remain untreated for years.

Cleansing the oral cavity

- Ayurveda is one of the earliest medical sciences to talk about the benefits, significance, medicinal herbs and method of brushing teeth which is as scientific as modern dental science. Gum care and tongue scrapping are two essential factors which only recently have been advertised by manufacturers of oral products.
- A dental cleanser should be fibrous but not too hard, to avoid injury to the gums. The cleansing medium should be mainly

astringent and bitter but including a little bit of sweetness. Kindly avoid toothpastes which are too sweet in taste.
- The usage of salt should be limited to gargling as it is an excellent cleanser for soft tissues (like gums, base of tongue, etc.) of the oral cavity but should not be rubbed into the teeth. Tongue cleaning is the best remedy for anyone suffering from bad breath or frequent throat infections as a lot of debris gets deposited there.

Oiling

- Our largest organ, the skin, like any other organ needs an all-around nutrition and since it is the seat of vata, external nutrition needs to be oil based since oil is the best way to pacify vata. No matter how many moisturizers one may use there is no substitute for pure natural oil.
- Oiling of the body is like a family tradition in India, for generations it has been used as a secret ingredient for beautiful skin and hair that Indians are known for in general. There is no better natural method to improve the tone of the body, increase vitality and vigour and decrease sensitivity to physical wear and tear.
- Oiling, ideally, should be done every day, if not, thrice a week in winters and twice in summers manages the body quite well.
- Still if you are time-pressed, the five points—naval, sole of feet, ears, head (in particular the soft spot), hands and elbows—should essentially be massaged with oil before taking bath. This should be a part of your daily or weekly routine and the earlier you start in life, the better it is for you.
- Sesame seed oil, olive oil, coconut oil, mustard oil and almond oil are beneficial for the body. Keep changing these over a period of two-three months. We will discuss more about their

seasonal utility in the *ritucharya* (seasons) chapter.

Nasyam

- *Nasyam* or clearing the nasal tract with herbal remedies is another easy-to-do, yet profound method of maintaining health. The nasal tract is the first entry point of air in our body, therefore it is the first to get exposed to dust, change in temperature, chemicals, etc. So, therefore it needs to be cleansed and nourished and nasyam is the way to do that. Many of you may remember how your grandmother used to insist on putting oil like almond oil (*badam rogan*), in the nostrils, especially during winters.
- This works exceptionally well because in winters the moisture content of air decreases so air gets dry and irritates the nasal tract, any other additional irritant like dust triggers allergic reaction causing allergic rhinitis (running nose) or allergic sinusitis (sinus, headache) which in further inflammation may lead to infection causing fever and aggravating the symptoms.
- You may have noticed in the month of October–November with the arrival of winter and end of autumn or in February–March upon arrival of spring many of us fall ill exhibiting these very symptoms. The best way to prevent this is to start applying Anu Thailam regularly in the morning and evening, one drop into each nostril thus conditioning and cleansing the nasal passage. Please remember to do this specially in the days of changing season. If you can make a habit if doing nasyam daily, it can easily lead to improved concentration and focus, proper breathing, as the nose is considered to be the door of the head in Ayurveda: '*nasa tu shirisho dwaram*'.

Humble water, your daily fix

- The Japanese have researched and published papers on the benefit of drinking water on an empty stomach, this easy-to-do detox chore is one of the mainstay of *panchmahabhoot chikitsha*, i.e. curing through the five elements.
- What is important to note here is that the quantity of water varies from person to person, also, from season to season. It was very difficult to change the mindset of my patients when the fashionable trend of drinking eight litres of water per day started spreading like a forest fire.
- One glass of water on empty stomach may be enough for Kapha prakriti people, one and a half glass is enough for vata predominant prakriti and pitta people can drink upto a litre of water at room temperature.
- Water stored overnight in a copper vessel works very well for people suffering from lack of energy. Warm water with lemon is not advised for people suffering from acidity. It might be a questionable trend for losing weight. I suggest drinking plain warm water to obese patients.
- Kindly avoid the vicious routine of bed tea by replacing it with cinnamon tea (dalchini) or fennel tea (saunf), then switch to warm water and consequently switch to a glass of plain water. Bed tea or coffee creates a havoc to the physiological system of the body, it is one of the easiest primary observed factor in people suffering from chronic acidity, obesity, dry cough, Vitamin B12 deficiency, dental issues, and even heart disease in some cases.

Workout

- Ayurveda puts a great emphasis on having a daily workout schedule for everyone, no matter what the age or sex is.

However, a person suffering from any kind of illness is exempted from this rule.

- Stretching, doing asanas, working out, walking, sexual activity and laughing are all examples of *vyayam*. Vyayam or exercise creates stability in the body and mind, resistance, flexibility, agility, lightness and hunger like no other.
- It provides a natural mechanism to the body to fight *Medhodusti,* which is related to leptin resistance. Leptin is the satiety hormone produced by fat cells in the body which maintains the amount of fat stored in the body. It does so by maintaining sensations of hunger and energy expenditure. In case of leptin resistance, the body slowly fails to respond to this mechanism, thus there is excessive hunger and haphazard energy expenditure resulting in excessive fat storage in the body. This is the vicious circle of obesity explained time and again in Ayurveda, albeit using Sanskrit terms. However, where there is a problem there is always a solution, if we are willing to take it.
- Exercise, yoga, walking are the first steps in this process. The ancient sages continuously cautioned about one arena of working out that exercise should use only half of your body's total strength.
- In case of panting, gasping for breath and over-perspiration, one should relax as stamina building should be a daily phenomenon.
- Over-exercise can lead to even bigger problems than under exercising. It may lead to weakness, excessive thirst, lethargy, allergic respiratory disorders, fever, bleeding from nose, etc. Exercising in evening or night time tends to increase vata (air element) in the body and should be avoided.

Bathing

- Many royals, not just of Indian origin, were very diligent about their bathing rituals; there are folklores of Cleopatra using goat's milk, rose and aloe vera for bathing. Many Ayurvedic texts contain substantial information about various combinations like sandalwood and milk or red sandal and milk, jasmine and champa or amla and reetha, etc. for bathing as some of those texts were written for rajas.
- Bathing in a way is a sensory pleasure, a meditative process, why only sit and meditate when it is meditation in motion. It is said in Sanskrit that it is ideal to bathe like an elephant, which loves water and enjoys it wholeheartedly.
- Water carries a lot of energy in it depending upon area of sourcing, like mountain water is very restorative in nature. Always check the temperature of water on legs first.
- The Vedic way of bathing suggests using water at higher temperature for area below the naval, at medium temperature for between the naval and shoulders and at a lower temperature for face and the head as these are areas of vata, pitta and kapha respectively.
- Alum is a very effective natural deodorizer and disinfectant which can be put in the water reservoir or using for sweat-prone areas.

Pranayama

- One of our most resplendent sciences, yoga, has been seen through the eyes of the western world which has embraced it and made it its own. Yoga means the realization of the union of the body and mind. All asanas are a part of yoga, however, yoga encompasses eight parts or angas that is why it is also called astanga yoga; asanas are only one part of that. These asanas should be done only to one's own capacity of flexibility and should be gradually increased in difficulty. The basic aim is to relieve stress on various sections by relieving pressure, stretching and relaxing. The accumulated toxins in even the minutest muscle mass of the body gets eliminated. The internal organs tend to release their secretions at appropriate time and, adequate quantity.

- *Pranayama* is the adept balance of prana and apana vayu i.e. energies on the top and bottom part of the body. This is achieved by practising rhythmic breathing exercises to ensure premium oxygenation of the body and eliminating toxins particularly from the respiratory and cardiac faculties of the body.
- *Dhyana* or meditation is neither contemplation nor concentration as is perceived by many. It is mere thoughtlessness of the mind. Upon emptying the mind, one achieves the control of losing the sense of self without going to sleep. It is silent awareness and dynamic peace of the mind. It can be done by everybody, with or without the help of a guru. It should be practised daily for at least 10 minutes in morning and in the evening.

Exfoliation

- *Uddavartanam* or *udhgarshanam* or ubtan has been an integral part of the ancient beauty regime. It is all the more important in cities today where the amount of sub-particulate is so high that it tends to get deposited between the pores of the skin thereby increasing the chances of blackheads, acne, etc. It should be done at least once a week.
- One of easiest uddavartanam pack is mixing chokker atta

(wholewheat) 1 part, oat Oats (1 part), turmeric (⅛ part), malai (½ part), coconut oil (½ part), aloe vera gel (optional, especially for acne-prone skin) (½ part) and rose water to keep the moisture intact. This should be applied with gentle, small circular motions and washed off after half an hour to get rid of blemishes, marks and unwanted hair.

Self-grooming

- Little things like combing, cutting nails and trimming hair are clearly mentioned in dinacharya (routine care) as even though they might seem like unimportant chores yet they end up defining the standard of hygiene and health.
- One might deduce that the substantial importance on personal hygiene Ayurveda has laid upon has a greater purpose than only outer beauty.
- 'Body is the temple of mind.' The realization of one's self and the realization of the higher self, both are going to be achieved through the medium of the physical body.
- Personal grooming instills a lot of personal confidence, good skin care and hair care regime makes the first impression. We live in a visual world where looking good (that too in a certain way defined by the latest fashion) is a sure-shot way of success by never-ending advertisements from cosmetic companies.
- It is actually the feel-good part, feeling settled in one's own body. Inner and outer radiance cannot be comparable to any cosmetic in the world.

Breakfast

- The most important meal of the day, what you have for breakfast ends up defining your whole day. Rushing to office, having breakfast while driving, eating while standing, all these

little things seem very unimportant during the daily chores but they make you carve for caffeinated drinks because of the lack of energy in the body due to an improper assimilation of breakfast.
- Food is a process of taking in energy from nature, it is the *bhautik* (physical) aspect of the energy chain, so if breakfast is hurried, there is unsatisfied craving for the bhautik that may linger on. Interestingly, bhautik also symbolizes consumerism. So not just from the food aspect, but one might also end up craving for materialistic things like a car, a dress or jewellery. You might end up making a totally irrational decision and taking a risk. Therefore, breakfast is important, very important.
- The ground rule here is to take something sweet in the morning and by sweet I do not mean an ice cream; I mean any food that has natural sugars but medium or low on glycaemic index. That means it should have an instant as well as slow release of glucose in the body to keep you active throughout the day.
- Sugar or *madhura rasa* is one that produces a sense of satiety and satisfaction. This feeling of completeness is required in the morning as the body has gone through required hours of fasting. Traditionally, having a sweet breakfast is known as *naivedyam* in south India and *kaleva* in northern India.
- There is potent *nuskha* (tip) that I advise all my patients and have seen marvellous results with—five almonds, one dry fig, one walnut and four raisins soaked for half an hour and to be eaten first thing in the morning. This combination is a sure-shot solution for vitamin deficiencies, cholesterol issues and works wonders for diabetics. People suffering from chronic back pain (after undergoing treatment for inflammation) can be maintained only on this formula and have seen great recoveries with this.

- Other breakfast superfoods include honey, ripened coconut, coconut water and oats. These should be included on and off in your diet. Please take care of the quantity of breakfast as it should be half or three-fourths of your full stomach. Avoid fried food in the morning as it might make you sleepy during the day.

Working towards your ultimate goal

- There is no medical science in the world that talks about the emphasis of working. The famous karma theory comprises not only the principle 'you shall reap what you sow' but also that 'karma is supreme'. The human being is bestowed with the largest brain among all living animals for this very purpose.
- We are here for a specific work, there are glorified examples how a single leader or single human might shape the world, or how a teacher might shape the life of a student or how a mother takes care of her child. Each and every effort is equally important as it is the little droplets that fill the ocean.
- There is a universal tradition of thanking God in case of something good happens and calling Him in case of something bad happens, both these calls are for the unknown. The unknown can be related to someone somewhere doing a deed that is of some good to you. The gratefulness is for this unknown karma. Therefore, every human on this planet must work. It doesn't necessarily state that every human must have a profession which pays him financially, yet he must work daily. Volunteer for the environment, feed the birds, water a plant or take care of an animal. These are all our responsibilities even if we don't feel responsible. Economic and social development without keeping these principles in policy have led to disasters.
- Karma theory also states that each work should be done

with undivided attention and diligence to achieve maximum efficiency. There is greatness waiting to unravel itself when work becomes meditation. If you do what you love and if you love what you do, there is unbounded creativity waiting for you. Multitasking (though quite famous nowadays) is not the ideal-case scenario. One thing must be done at a time. There is no substitute for training and discipline as fortune indeed favours the brave.
- The word yoga has been described in the Bhagavad Gita as *yogah to karmasu kaushalam,* i.e. doing each work with absolute skill is yoga. So working with a restful mind makes one a yogi.

Lunch

- The part of midday when sun comes on top of the head is pitta kaal and, therefore, this is the time when the human body feels most hungry as pitta inside also gets aggravated.
- Lunch should be the principal meal of the day. It is said that we should eat breakfast like a king, lunch like a common man and dinner like a pauper. However, the best practice is to make lunch the most nutritious meal of the day which should comprise of protein (dal, etc.), carbohydrates, greens (spinach, etc.), salads (steamed/baked) and yoghurt. Check the quantity so as to retain the activeness of body and mind.

Evening schedule

- To snack or not to snack? This is a very interesting thought that crosses through the mind of weight-watchers almost every hour of the day. Yes, our brain needs continuous supply of glucose that is derived from food as it is a high-energy expenditure organ. Therefore, I say don't snack, take refreshments.
- It is okay to feel a tad bit hungry in between meals but what

you eat in this snacking time is very crucial in maintaining a healthy body. The food needs to refresh you not burden you.
- Chaach (very thin skimmed yoghurt with water, cumin/coriander powder), fruit bowl, Ayurvedic makhana mix, bhoona chana and salads are examples of good refreshments.
- It is our physical need for hot water that is somehow substituted with addictive habits of consuming tea and coffee. I have noticed many a times that there are families who drink tea and families who don't. This bias of the modern Indians is that of mild addiction and most addictions are initiated to give company. Similarly, there are offices where coffee rounds are very common and are like tools of social networking.
- However, this trend is changing slowly because leaders of many organizations are also opting for the benefits of herbal tea and green teas. Still, there is no substitute for hot water. Water boiled for 20 minutes is the best medicine that is easily and universally available.
- Our lives consist more travelling and more mental work than our previous generations. Both these things tend to increase restlessness in the body. Let me mention here that evening is the second-best time to meditate in the day, the ideal time to get worries out of your head and body, and to move towards a relaxed night-time regime. Splashing rose water on face and drinking a glass of hot water are two wonderful evening rituals.

Dinner

- The time when one takes dinner is the definitive marker of the standard of one's health. The later one eats dinner, the unhealthier he is. Therefore, early dinner is a basic rule for having a great morning thereafter. Unfortunately, not many people follow this; and moreover, late working hours, extended

travel time due to traffic congestions have further postponed the time of dinner for the working families.
- Kindly avoid dinner altogether if it is just an hour before your bedtime as it may postpone or hinder your sleep altogether. Ideal situation calls for a difference of at least two hours between sleep and dinner.
- The quantity should be the least of the day, just enough to curb your hunger. At no instance overfeed yourself at dinner time as this habit is the mainstay for developing obesity, dyslipidaemia, cardiac issues and sleep disorders.
- Vegetable soup, semi-cooked salads and simple carbs like subzis are quintessential to a healthy dinner. Eat only a single grain and that too in the least possible quantity like one or two chapattis (depends upon body weight).
- Avoid vata aggravating or gassy foods like rajma, urad dal (both black and yellow), chole, etc. in the dinner. These are good foods to be consumed in breakfast or lunch.

Sleep

- Sleep is one of the most important pillars of human body; it is required for holding most of the physiological functions of the human body. Sleep can be defined as losing one's sense of self. This happens when the consciousness or the knowledge of identity is lost which is gained back when you get up.
- Sleep is considered tamasic in nature, this has a lot of deep meanings and sleep is essential cleaning the system of the body, to clean anything one has to get his hands dirty that is what tamas is. So sleep is the loss of awareness which is, in fact, essential for the body to achieve detoxification, rejuvenation and growth.
- There are various kinds of sleep like arising by nature

(*swabhavam*) that is due to absence of sun, this is basic and is quintessential, others being due to negative feelings (*papma*), due to increased kapha, due to increased workout of body and mind, due to any disease, a way for healing. This means that your body will require more sleep if you are under stress or are recuperating from any disease.

- Many psychological issues have been linked to sleep deprivation by modern-day researchers. Ayurveda has linked many psychosomatic disorders with sleep deprivation, as it has aggravated a lot of vata. Illness accompanied with pain is seen in patients with years of sleep deprivation.
- As for the hours of sleep required by the body, it may vary between seven to nine hours as kapha prakriti people especially children tend to sleep more, what is more important is the time of deep sleep which is just about two hours, this deep sleep is even more beneficial if it's taken before midnight i.e. if you sleep by 10 p.m. at night.
- The benefits of proper sleep are innumerable. Adequate deep sleep improves memory and cognitive functions, streamlines physiology, promotes weight loss in overweight individuals on the contrary promotes healing in ailing people promotes happiness makes body light and energizes it.
- Always remember to sleep more when you are going through any illness because a good sleep well does half of the healing work in the body. There are several available researches that also enlighten us upon this important part of life, deep sleep allows the release of growth hormone in the body which is responsible for growth, healing and reversing the ageing process.
- There is a common query that I face that even after following strict diet fads with dedication, there is no significant weight loss or inch loss from the body. This is because of not sleeping

properly! So if you are following any workout regimen kindly take sleeping hours into your routine as sleep increases both endurance and perseverance of the body.

- There are many natural ways to enhance sleep quality like having a light and early dinner, having half a cup of warm milk just before sleeping and massaging your feet with sesame seed oil. These will make you sleep well and pave way for a beautiful sunrise both outside and inside the body.

Wise is the person, who takes care of himself,
Like a charioteer does for a chariot or a ruler should do
for his city.
For body is the temple where the real deity resides, take care!

Chapter Three

Ayurveda for Every Season

The environment is a very specific, cyclic and coordinated turn of climatic events. This cycle affects the soil, crops and even the population. If you cannot wear the same kind of clothes throughout the year, how can you eat the same kind of food? There is no medical science that gives a detailed explanatory health regime for specific parts of the year called 'ritucharya' which is basically seasonal regimen to be observed throughout a ritu (season). A ritu is a specific period comprising of two months and in total there are six ritus in the year, this is more specific in comparison to the four seasons followed as per western culture i.e. spring, summer, autumn and winter.

It is the movement of the Earth with respect to the sun that ascertains these following divisions of the year. A lot of time was spent on studying the movement of celestial objects in Vedic era, as it provided the time guidelines for farming, travel, etc. Hence there were accurate divisions of the time with relations to the sun and the moon vis-à-vis the effect upon us. The year is divided into two kaals:

1. Adaan Kaal—when sun is nearer to the Earth
2. Visharg Kaal—when the sun is getting away from the Earth

Being an agricultural community, it was noticed that these changes had a great effect on crops as well as humans.

There is always a tendency in everyone to fall sick in a particular time of the year, some blame it on the weather, some blame it on the flu; nobody notices that the environment is literally showing signals to change your daily routine, the sun is at different setting, he is the ultimate provider, change your timings and routine accordingly. If you follow this prescribed regimen in the previous season, after which you generally tend to fall sick, I assure you that your trip to doctor will be only to greet him on festivals. To elaborate further, if you fall sick in February-March, especially follow the regime for December–January as it is in these very months that your body is accumulating toxins. Or, if the festive season of October–November gives you trouble every time that means you did not take care of your body during monsoon. This is a very interesting fact as we seldom look at ourselves in this way. To all of you who go for 'every two month' service of your car, how often do you get yourself serviced? Have you checked your internal oil levels?

Dryness or *rukhsta* in the body is very common nowadays. Extreme continuous dryness is one of the basic causative factors for imbalance, if left untreated it can lead to severe restlessness and other vayu imbalances. You do take holidays once in a while to rest but on the contrary, vacations are even more stressful than normal days, too much travelling, too much vata, when do you restore and rejuvenate yourself?

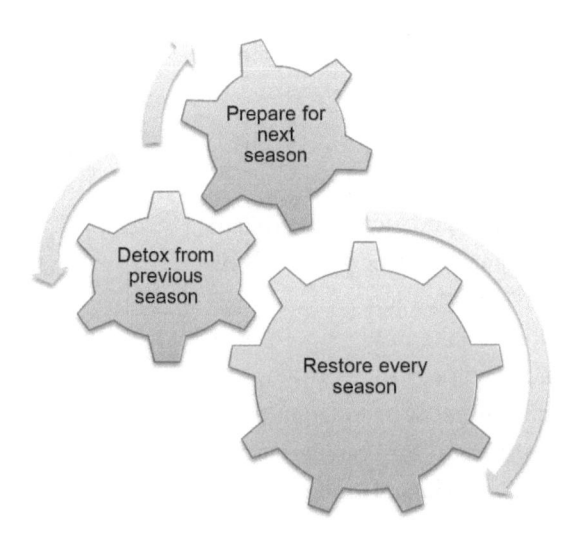

The basic principle of seasonal regimen

SHISHIRA RITU

Since our official year is based on the Roman calendar, I will start the description with the beginning of the year, the *shishira ritu* or winter. In the winter season, nature is in kind of a slumber and so are we; there is increased craving for caffeine and other hot beverages. The hot beverages part is very much required for the body but caffeine is not.

A 60-day period of extreme winter wave in the northern hemisphere starts from 15 December goes on till 15 February, there is certain nip in the air, air is very cold and dry with hardly any sun. This extremely sharp and cool air creates a response in our body in which our agni (digestive fire) lights up, the freezing temperature persists and deposits kapha element in the body.

The internal effect on the body is that you have an increased appetite; you need to increase complex carbs and proteins in your diet. There is also a tendency to have improper cleansing or sometimes constipation. So it is better to take mild laxatives in that case.

Season/Ritu	Shishira
Time	Mid-December–Mid-February
Western Analogue	Late winter
Doshas	Kapha+

Fasting is not recommended in this season and skipping meals because the increased agni can even exploit the tissue system of the body thus leading to loss of immunity and increased risk of fever, etc.

Eating food that is cold and dry, can lead to gastric issues and not protecting the body against the harsh wind can lead to bodyaches, especially joints, and dry, itchy skin and breathing issues. Pitta people might suffer from watery motion so it is better to take isabgol with curd in the morning in this case.

The prescribed diet throughout these months is of freshly made, properly spiced seasonal veggie serving at least two times a day. There is a plethora of seasonal veggies like spinach, carrots, beetroot, methi leaves, bathua leaves, etc. It is also a time to explore grains like ragi (finger millet) and bajra, as khichdi or daliya.

The food substance should be sour, bitter and astringent to counter the kapha in the body. Non-vegetarians should take meals in form of soups and these should be prepared with ample amount of veggies as the body is able to assimilate it better that way.

Please don't exclude oils entirely from your diet as the body's requirement of daily fat goes up because of the arid climate. *Ghritam* (ghee) should not be used for deep frying but used be used as a garnish for proteins like dals and complex carbs like roti. Sesame seed oil is like a boon in this season both for local application and cooking. Mustard oil, canola oil, olive oil are also very useful as they because of their potency.

Avoid sleeping during the daytime. Eating at an improper time or eating before the previous meal has been digested can be problematic for the stomach. Do not eat without any hunger and improvise on your water intake as you might not feel that thirsty. This time of year is the best for stamina building, culminating immunity and developing 'ojas' (resolute equilibrium) for the physical body. Therefore, exercise regularly; do stretching at least three times a day for seven to eight minutes.

Detox in the winter season by sunbathing, regular intake of hot water and using spices like black pepper, big cardamom, saffron, cloves, chives, garlic, tejpatta (bay leaf) nutmeg, mace, star anise, long pepper or pippali, saunth or dry ginger, fenugreek seeds (methidana) provide ample protection from seasonal infections.

Seasonal home remedies are amla chutney, liquorice (mulethi) tea and turmeric milk. Grate raw turmeric and put in cold milk and bring to boil; similarly saffron milk and date milk can be prepared. Quite a few recipes in chapter six are apt for this season.

This is the time to increase meditation and avoid conflicts, winters brings a sense of negativity with it. So keep yourself jovial and do social work as much as you can. The rate of depression or negative episodes shoots up in this season; it is the time to learn to be patient and to work hard. Be thankful to the sun and the fire, without which it is very tough to survive in cold conditions.

VASANT RITU

Winter makes way for spring and nature wakes up to its beautiful splendour with the season of colour. The flowers bloom, birds chirp and sing, making it beautiful outdoors. The days start to get longer than the nights. This season is the best time to take out vitiated kapha from the body.

This is the best time to take detox therapies. The accumulated kapha throughout previous two months sources an outlet in these months. If this regimen is not followed, there is an increased risk of developing breathing allergies, skin diseases and high-grade fever. The time range is from middle of February to the middle of April. It is the busiest time of the year for academicians, finance professionals and doctors.

Symptoms that tend to occur due to change in weather are loss of appetite, nausea and possible vomiting, heaviness in the body, pallor of the skin, cold hands and feet, joint pains, cough with phlegm, excessive sleep, lethargy and lack of concentration. Incorporation of ginger, cinnamon, garlic, asafoetida (hing), green chillies and mustard oil in the daily diet will be beneficial. Oils should be preferred more than ghee.

Season/Ritu	Vasant
Time	Mid-February–Mid-April
Western Analogue	Spring
Doshas	Kapha++

The seasonal regimen for spring season or vasant ritu, if followed, not only prevents the above mentioned disorders but also alleviates the root cause of any diseases. Cold, oily and heavy foods like yoghurt, cheese, butter, red meat and cucumber and melons should be avoided.

Buttermilk should act as substitute for curd. Milk with cinnamon and cardamom is very soothing to the body. Honey is beneficial in this season and should be taken daily first thing in the morning.

This is the most common time when viral infections proliferate in huge number. It is better to avoid unctuous food completely like fried items, ice creams, too salty or too sweet things. Take lukewarm water regularly. It is better to completely cover oneself even if not with woollens. Maintain a regular exercise schedule.

Avoid grains in large quantity, abstain from rice and stick to wheat (to be eaten in smaller quantities). Gourds make the best veggies to eat along with all peppers. Bitter gourd, striped gourd (parwal), pointed gourd and moong dal are to be used like staple items. The rule is to take hot and fresh food with pungent, bitter, and astringent tastes. For increasing digestion, ginger, black pepper and turmeric should be used. Five to six black pepper seeds first thing in an empty stomach in the morning is an effective detoxification method.

Pamper yourself; it is the time for exfoliation of the skin, along with hot oil massage and sauna bath. Body should be massaged with light aromatic oils. While taking a sauna always cover your head, eyes and chest area with a damp cloth to avoid overheating of these parts. Generously apply almond oil or sesame seed oil to the inside of the nostrils to condition the air and to avoid pollen allergies.

Panchakarma therapies like *vamana* and *shiro-virechana* should be done to annihilate toxins from the body. As there is an increase in the feeling of excessive greed and attachment (marketed as the season to fall in love), the mind also, simultaneously, gets effected. So, pranayama should be done to achieve internal cleansing.

GRISHMA RITU

The sun starts to become shinier and brighter and brings a lot of joy and positivity with it. The grishma ritu or summer season starts from the second half of April and lasts till mid of June. This time days become longer and more fruitful.

It is the best time to start a new mental exercise but abstain from rigorous physical exercise as the body should not undergo any stress if you start working out in a gym at this time of the year. You may end up leaving it without any reason whatsoever. The sun's heat becomes stronger every day, evaporates water from the Earth and from our body. This process causes an accumulation of vayu in the body. There is an increased amount of energy in the mind whereas the physical strength decreases.

Swimming is the only exercise prescribed due to excessive thirst and sweating. Yoga and Pilates can also be done regularly. The digestive fire or agni starts to decrease and therefore sour and sweet items should be consumed.

Delightful fruits such as amla, kokum and mango grow in this season, providing a lot of options to make the palette extremely healthy and colourful. Melons, cucumber, watermelon, grapes, pomegranate and coconut replenishes the aqua cycle of the body. This is the season to consume rice and wheat.

Season/Ritu	Grishma
Time	Mid-April–Mid-June
Western Analogue	Summer
Doshas	Vata+

Avoid roasted foods as they tend to dry up the body and vitiate both vata and pitta. Stop your dry fruit intake. Non-vegetarians should abstain from meat, eggs and may switch to fresh seafood. Avoid alcohol in this season as it increases heat in the body and dehydrates intrinsic tissue of the body beyond measure.

Reduce garlic in the diet and replace spices with coriander

(leaves and seeds), mint, onion, cumin, fennel seeds, curry leaves, green cardamom, poppy seeds, anardana (pomegranate seeds), etc. Basically, you need to change your spice basket. Ghee and rice bran oil or coconut oil should be used in moderate quantity. Home-made chaach should be consumed daily and it is a great accompaniment for the office.

Skin pores begin to open, therefore bathing with aromatic oils is refreshing. Chandana, khus and bhrami are great for internal and external use. Soaking coriander seeds overnight and taken in the morning is a great home remedy to combat excessive heat, dates with milk, rose water with buttermilk are great coolants. Pure rose-petal preserve or gulkanda is a great way to start the day.

It is the only season of the year when day-sleeping is advised, so stretch your body on a fixed time during the day and go for a power nap else lethargy may creep in. Bathe with aromatic bath salts and wear loose and fragrant clothing.

Be cautious as this is also the time when gastric diseases build up in the body and there is an increased rate of digestive disorders like diarrhoea, therefore all rehydration solutions should be kept at bay. Coconut water should also be consumed at least once a week to maintain ionic balance in the body.

VARSHA RITU

Varsha is the season of our beloved monsoon, when rains quench the thirst of Mother Earth and fill our environment with the fragrance of aqua. Rainwater strikes the hot Earth and creates a lot of water vapour in the atmosphere, thus ending up increasing the moisture content in the air. There is an increase in the acidity of water of the environment which is seen when fresh water rivers are highly polluted at this time of the year.

Keep yourself hydrated because in the preceding summer month the body has been dehydrated, so lack of the water element produces increase of air element in the body and the water vapour coming from the Earth along with increased acidity of soil and water increases the heat element of the body.

Season/Ritu	Varsha
Time	Mid-June–Mid-August
Western Analogue	Monsoon
Doshas	Vata++ Pitta+

In other words, vayu gets vitiated and pitta gets accumulated in the body. Therefore a strict regimen of moderate food intake is advised. There is an evident weakness in the digestive system; however, one may crave for salty and sour dishes which may be taken in small quantities.

Avoid curd, maida-based (flour) products like bread, biscuit, pizza, etc., as it gets accumulated in the gut. It is time to cut out fast food and take freshly cooked home-made food. This is time to eat barley or oats along with wheat and rice in moderate quantities. Excessive protein diet will also not be suitable at this time of the year. Therefore, vegetarians should abstain from cheese and big legumes such as urad and rajma. Non-vegetarians should, at this time, abstain from their usual habits as meat or fish may carry toxic pollutants (even lead) from the environment which can play havoc to the liver and the intestines.

Detoxify your body during the period of June (second half) to August (first half). The lunar month of sharavan or saavan comes in this season which is associated with a lot of fasting days. This is indeed a time to detox and one of the best months to do panchakarma. It is said in Ayurveda that if panchakarma is done at this time of the year annually, one will be nourished from the roots like a well-rooted tree. When you do not water the root of the tree it will eventually get dry and lifeless. So this is the time for *vasti karma* that is to moisturize the root of your body to keep it youthful. Vasti karma is medicated enema made of Ayurvedic aushadh which is to be done under the guidance of an astute physician.

Excessive sunlight, exorbitant exercises, indulgent sleeping, unnecessary eating are all condemned. It is the month for moderation in everything. Avoid intake of icy-cold liquid or food, abstain from day-time sleeping and staying up at night. The immunity of body is low at this time so there is tendency for acute infections; kindly take water which is lukewarm or at room temperature.

Food regimen should include ghee, which can be consumed in small quantities, and sesame seed oil or til tailam is the best suited cooking medium and great for application on skin. Curried vegetables are the best home-made eatables. Prefer taking buttermilk with asafoetida and ginger. You should consume puffed rice or poha and upma or liquid semolina. Keep dinner very light and don't exercise at night. Harar or haritaki is one of the best herbs to take in this season and its dried version is easily available in the market. The famous *hingaavastaka choorna* and *dashmoolaristam* can be taken by both adults and kids to keep vata at bay.

Special monsoon care should be taken which includes foot care; using proper shoes and umbrella, and wearing ironed (non-damp) clothes is advisable. Pamper your skin with ubtans or lepas to avoid dryness and infection. Monsoon causes a lot of hair loss in patients, which is again a combination of extrinsic and intrinsic factors. Try to keep your hair clean and dry. Excessive shampooing makes hair brittle and water sources are adulterated in this period, hair will end up getting dirty pretty often. Therefore, it is better to wash the hair once a week with natural substances like multani mitti, curd and reetha–shikakai. Oil your hair regularly, albeit in the night and wash in the morning. Nasyam with anu thailam is a very effective therapy for hair fall or headache; put one drop for each nostril thrice daily for wonderful results.

SHARAD RITU

This season is the perennial conjunction of the seasonal divide from summer to winter. This is about welcoming change which is both internal and external. There is a gradual decrease in sunshine and rainfall. However, the sun is very strong, but body is accustomed to the cooling effect of rain. Therefore, there is reduction of moisture in the body, surrounding with an increased heat element. This results in the vitiation of pitta.

Note that this is the time to avoid anything that increases acidity in the body. It is the season of the year to take the least amount of salt. Stay away from spicy delicacies. Pickles are to be completely avoided. The consumption of alcohol is avoided for sharadam as it exorbitantly vitiates pitta.

Changes may show in the body due to varied appetite which increases gradually in the latter half of the season. The time ranges from the end of August to October. It is the time to eat small nutritive foods throughout the day. Food should be sweet, light, lukewarm and balanced with spices like cinnamon, fennel,

Season/Ritu	Sharad
Time	Mid-August–Mid-October
Western Analogue	Autumn
Doshas	Pitta++

cumin, coriander, mint, asafoetida, black pepper, etc. Reduce the amount of chilly in the food during this time which you can increase in the following months.

Abstain from garlic and gorge on astringent substances like gooseberry. Warm zucchini salad, with moong dal (yellow gram) and shaali rice (non-polished rice) is an example of an ideal lunch. Green moong or green dal, ragi with buttermilk, wheat with gourds like gheeya (bitter gourd) and parwal (striped gourd) are suitable options. Seafood and curd are again to be avoided. Warm stewed apple in the morning with cinnamon is an example of a breakfast or snack recipe. People of pitta prakriti should exercise extra caution during this season, the buildup in the intestines may cause acidity or indigestion and may even flare up an episode of piles.

Seasonal home remedies include a drink of aloe vera; however it is not advisable for children and pregnant women. It will help to take excessive heat out from the body. Therapeutic intestinal cleansing or virechana is the best therapy. Make a rule to take water on an empty stomach or you can leave water outside with a couple of cinnamon sticks throughout the night exposed to moon rays and take it first thing in the morning. It is a great way to realize how the energy of water can soothe our body. We should use room temperature water for drinking and cool water for bathing. Swimming is a good exercise for this season. An early morning walk is a therapy in itself. Mild intestinal cleansers like raisins, triphala, isabgol or papaya can be taken once every week to keep toxins to the minimum.

HEMANT RITU

This is the season of early winter, with the cold knocking at your door step! This ritu starts from the latter half of October and carries on till the mid of December. With the weather changing to winter, body also undergoes a change.

Internally, the digestive fire, which has been on the lower side during the preceding varsha and sharad ritus, slowly starts to increase, with hunger strongly increasing in the

Season/Ritu	Hemant
Time	Mid-October–Mid-December
Western Analogue	Early winter
Doshas	Balanced

morning. Also the vitiated pitta decreases on its own, naturally, so one's problem with acidity will tend to decrease.

This is one time of the year when you should never skip your breakfast. This is the best time of the year to start a workout regime. The body which is undergoing a positive change will get easily accustomed to any workout requirements. All grains should be slowly encouraged into the diet in increasing quantities with adequate lentils and vegetables. You can slowly increase salt and spice in your diet as the body is able to utilize it well. Take a mixture of five power foods in the morning, comprising six almonds, one fig, five raisins, one walnut and one date. Take servings of herbal tea twice in the day to regulate the appetite and to keep cravings at bay.

Start massaging the body with oil at least thrice a week or if you can manage to do daily, it will be all the more beneficial. The fact that the Indian wedding season coincides with this season is both amusing and scientific. You do require extra energy and effort to go to a whole lot of weddings and also you might be able to digest the food better compared to other weddings or parties at different time of the year. So please make sure that you have one principle meal one time of the day and this should not be at night.

Therefore, lunch again becomes very important.

Avoid fasting or dieting during this period, even though this is the best time to lose weight. So eating at fixed timings with a balanced diet will easily lead to losing weight and inches too. Some people might face breathing allergies due to changing season and pranayama is an effective preventive measure. The strength of the body or *vyadhikshamtava* is something that is built just by natural means. So if you give it a little boost, it will eventually lead to disease-free holiday season with more productivity and creative intelligence.

These all are in cyclic motion so one has to carefully change from one to another. The way to a peaceful and disease-free life is to slowly leave the regimen of the previous season by letting go of one meal per day and slowly inculcating the coming regimen by including one habit per day. This 15-day period is called *hritusandhi* or the conjunction of ritus and it is the time frame of 15 days comprising seven days of the ritu that went by and seven days of the coming ritu.

The Newtonian theory of action and equal reaction can be related in the present context, just as there are continuous changes in the environment body (in the response to an external stimuli) changes. However, many of us do not follow this, for them Ayurveda says that they have been habituated to these stubborn habits like the body gets habituated to slow poisoning i.e. *aaksatyam*. One gets so used to all these toxins that the feeling of being perpetually ill becomes a norm and the habit of popping a pill every now and then becomes a weekly ritual. It becomes a prakriti of the body, even though in normal conditions these might be harmful for you.

Remember to utilize Ayurveda for every season and adopt Ayurveda for every reason.

Chapter Four

Ayurveda for Work Life

The sudden shift in life comes when the soft belly, which used to digest everything in school and college, suddenly undergoes a slowdown. Just as the flourishing economies are bound to undergo recession at some point in time, our body, no matter how fit, tends to go under a digestive and metabolic recession when a sedentary life sets in. Our modern-day lives have become a jargon about managing things, managing work and looking after the family. In this mayhem, we forget to manage ourselves, thus making a big blunder because all management starts from one's self. This chapter is not about philosophy, but is the gist of real-time discussions I have had with my patients coming from a corporate background and the nuances I have noticed after organising numerous health camps at major corporates.

When I am given a random set of people from a corporate firm, it is very clear to identify their work by the condition of their *nadi*. Nadi is a Sanskrit word originating from the word 'naad' meaning primordial sound, and *nadiparikhshan* is a method by which a trained medical practitioner or *vaidya* is able to assess the internal condition of a person by analyzing his nadi, that is his energy. This is done by reading of the pulse in an Ayurvedic way. So coming back to assessing the nadi of a few corporate, I have noted that the extremely stressed, as if living on the edge, are the people from the sales and marketing department. These are already driven individuals who are given targets and deadlines like no other, they travel the most, and hence their health tends to suffer the most. Next are the ones from IT, who are the most sleep deprived of the lot, and probably need to be the most innovative. However, their lack of mental rest is big hindrance for them. The people from HR and administration are a mixed bag, from the cream at the top who are like focused sharks who take good care of themselves, to the executive staff who are running around like confused, tamed sheep in a herd. It sure is ironical that the part of the workforce which is the best paid hardly invests any time on themselves. This is a summary of the solutions that have worked for a large number of people over a long course of time, all finding their source in the Vedic way of living life. It is about serving an old, wonderfully aged wine in a snazzy new bottle. Human beings have evolved in a lot of ways; however, the root cause of all problems and the simple solution to them broadly remains the same.

So the paradigm is set that the professional atmosphere nowadays is stressed across the board. This fact has been established but exactly why needs to be understood. And what are the solutions to decrease stress levels? Are the solutions feasible for a time-pressed lifestyle?

The answer to all the above questions is not standard but rather explanatory, the same solution to manage health will not work for individuals with different work criterions. However, throughout the course of the chapter, you will find the answers best suitable for you, which will fit perfectly in your lifestyle provided you have the intention to make changes in your lifestyle.

In any sphere of work one is not allowed to lose focus and needs to be 100 per cent efficient all the time; one mistake may cost you a negative performance appraisal or the loss of trust. Sometimes it is easy to get away with a mistake but that only happens sometimes. Fortune not only favours the brave, but luck is created by minimizing the negatives and maximizing the positives. Therefore, fortune favours the efficient.

The unending race

There has to be a constant, comfortable and effortless transition between isolation and team work if you wish got to be successful at workplace. One needs to constantly change roles, because it is, in fact, a race, in which you are running for yourself. First, let's focus on individuality, ways to improve individual efficiency then we will emphasis on team management, from core to periphery.

You must have heard the commonest phrase: It is lonely on the top. How and when does it get lonely, I ask? Was it lonely from the time you started or did it become lonely in the journey because you let it be that way. It is true that there is a part of us that requires isolation; there are ways to look at it. It is also true that humans are not meant to be together always because of certain mental qualities that exist in all of us. I think it is best to be truthful to ourselves first about our qualities and shortcomings like selfishness, competition, ego and many other traits. First accept yourself as who you are, and, therefore, accept people and situations as they are. Just as it is difficult to change the mould you have set yourself in, it is impossible to change the others. What unites us then? It is the sense of a common purpose. When you see a great work done understand that there would have been problems and conflicts in the way. Hence it is the purpose that unites us, not themselves alone. The virtue of commitment is one of the positive qualities of a human beings. But that commitment needs to be towards work so that it therefore will serve a larger purpose for a longer period of time. Please remember that we species are meant to be *karmapradhan*, we have been blessed with greater intelligence to do work, one should never ever lose the sense of this responsibility that we have towards ourselves as human beings that we have to constantly work; not for money, not for your boss, but just for yourself. We have to get inspired by nature all the time. The sun cannot take a single day of absence; it may take a small vacation behind the clouds but is constantly working.

Vedic motivation is to have a purpose (dharma), to not get worried while doing action (karma) or expecting the reward. One may wonder how this applies to the modern scenario where fatter pay cheques, higher incentive, sponsorships are the driving force across all industries. Contrary to the popular belief this monetary, statistics tell a different story. Economists have researched that higher incentives does not necessarily prompt to positive impact in productivity. In fact, it leads to negative impact, with higher attrition due to increased competition and higher failure rate. With eyes on the prize, one is just distracting the mind from the actual targets of the work itself.

It is not tough to notice that most recent success stories of technology be it Google, Facebook or Twitter (and many more) is all free for the user. Even the most successful mobile applications, gaming or otherwise, start as free and later have additional paid plug-ins. They invite and engage before payment and thus end up earning more. What is the incentive here? It is the engagement the user gets out of the experience. One may use this example of the general population in the workspace. As people's managers one should look for engagement rather than hierarchical formalities. In the present scenario where idea and innovation have become the basic rule of the game, expression should not be curbed in name of formal multinational culture. The Vedas sing praises of the guru, but also describe how an ideal guru or leader should be a good observer, an astute listener and an epitome of compassion. The more engaged you and your colleague or employee is in the work, the more productivity it will lead to. A classic choice is between a horse and a fish. Do you want to be at horse at work or a fish? The horse represents power and strength, all factors attributing to high aptitude. There is a very famous technique of increasing mechanical activity in the function of a horse if a carrot is tied to limit his vision and (may be beaten with a stick) so that he runs fast on a straight track, and runs continuously because he doesn't look in the periphery, as it is lured by the thought of catching the carrot. He will eventually finish the race, may even win it. But the horse becomes a trained pet and not an innovator or leader and may ram into an obstacle which it may not foresee. The end result is optimum mechanical activity with promise of incentive which is very a cruel approach. Whereas success is akin to swimming like a fish, the deeper and calmer the dive is, the beautiful the scenario can get. The fish movement is constant, untiring, beautiful, minimum in effort, yet some of the fastest creatures on the Earth happen to be fish because they can go with the flow, yet create their own way.

Harness your talent

Excellence doesn't come by birth. By harnessing the unique ability of our mind which everyone possesses, one will be able to carve a niche for self in a fast-changing world. After achieving excellence within ourselves, success comfortably follows you around. The art of having a unique skill was praised by the ancient kings to modern CEOs, how to harness maximum efficiency for the longest period is the question everyone needs an answer to. We will solve this puzzle in this chapter. Man is a highly efficient machine; so quite a handful of inspiration lies within you and many of the life-changing experiences can come from everyday jobs like taking care of your children or your parents.

The regimen

For surviving in the jungle of corporate politics, be a little strict with yourself; listen to your body and follow a routine tailor-made for you. A routine that should comprise a clear bowel in the morning, followed by exercise, yoga and meditation, a nice shower, a healthy breakfast and five minutes of wholesome entertainment be it listening to music or dancing to a song. Once you land up a dream job, you cannot let yourself go.

Posture

The human body with its complex muscular skeletal system has been designed for maximum physical efficiency. No extent of evolution or civilization can alter this basic programming of nature. This clearly suggests that no one should be sitting continuously for more than eight hours. Continuous sitting has been related with increased rate of mortality irrespective of your during a workout or some physical activity at another time of the day. Always remember to take regular breaks from your desk to move around and stretch. This is extremely important. Remember to walk up to a colleague's desk instead of using the intercom or help the office staff by making your own cup of tea for a change. Arm stretching, upper body stretches, deep breathing, cyclic chanting should done in five min break every hour.

While sitting align your back with the seat of the chair as they are designed in that way that the back should be relaxed. It should be straight with shoulders held back in natural state so that as to make a straight line with the floor, your weight evenly distributed on the buttocks and upper thighs.

While standing for a long time, change standing position quite often, always straighten your back while standing up after sitting for a long period of time, walk with a correct posture with chin tucked in and toes pointing forward.

While lifting objects always bend your knees and not your back to get into a lower position, most of injuries occur while lifting objects. While carrying loads keep them as close to the body. For women who wear heels always carry a pair of spare flats in your car/locker and yes, wear heels only when required to do so because, as suggested by uncountable researches, they can play havoc to your spinal support.

While driving take sufficient time to drive so that you don't get agitated on your way to work in case of an unavoidable traffic jam. It is better to be five minutes late than get your car rammed into another one. Always support your lower back while driving for a long period of time by keeping a soft pillow or rolling up a towel and try to sit up straight. The driver's seat should be at such an angle so that the knees are in level with the line of the hips as it is the most comfortable for foot movement.

Diet

Do not compare yourself with other specially in terms of eating. The diet of the office runner will be and should be very different from that of a manager or anybody who has a sitting job. As I have already discussed before, just as all are facial structures are different so are our internal physiological structures. Everybody requires a different quantity to eat and different amount of time to digest. Research has also suggested that the freebies provided by any company tend to go off the shelves sooner than estimated quantity. This is not just an extra expense on the company but an extra load on the body as well because the body with limitless potential has a limited energy which can be either used in digesting an overstuffed gut or using an over-stressed mind.

Caffeine intake may provide the essential kick-start to the day, but where there is already eight months of summer, on top of that caffeine will lead to excessive sweating, interferes with digestion and being a diuretic will lead to loss of electrolytes if taken excessively. Interestingly, the tea plant is not native to India, in the colonization process, the British the farmers of the hills were forced to cultivate tea, now India has become one of largest consumers of tea in the world and our version (milk mixed with sugar) has the worst effect on teeth, stomach and what not. Similarly, the culture of drinking coffee on an empty stomach has been introduced off late by the multinationals, which is even more addictive than tea. Usually, these kinds of habits are taken up to just merely follow superiors from international locations.

Refrain from drinking caffeine/soft drinks after your lunch as it will interfere with the absorption of the food you just ate. If possible, take a walk or stretch after your lunch or do foot stretching exercises on your chair only to freshen yourself.

Routine

Set up a body clock in coordination with your work clock. For a normal day at work eat at a regular time every day and have the same schedule for the team. Our body has exceptional sensors in terms of chemical hormones, which triggers response in stressful situations if it is not fed on time. There are some offices where if the schedule of the leader is irregular in terms of timings, the whole team follows suit. Even if you are just one team member try to set a culture of discipline and time management, and, believe me, it all starts from food only.

Scaling the peak, one stair at a time

Climbing is a great exercise that can be done at any time. Make climbing the stairs an important component of your work life; you can set a limited number of floors according to your time and stamina. It will help you burn calories and aid in the movement of hips, upper thighs and knees making it an ideal exercise for someone who sits all day. It is actually a much better exercise than running as running tends to put stress on the knee, hence a more appropriate option for anyone with knee pain. Every once in a while climb two stairs at a time to tone up those calf muscles.

Power of power nap

Sleep deprivation is the major hindrance of the corporate work life, the yearning and dependency on caffeine is the result and the accelerator of this vicious circle of lack of sleep. Power nap comes in handy and charges the body. This skill requires a bit of training, do it for the same time frame of 15 minutes once a day, if you have the time and space to do it. It is actually just meditation in *shavasana* because it is a mind-training technique; it has been given a fancy name and works well for a majority of working people across the globe. It improves concentration, productivity and efficiency. Some international organizations also give out specific time for these methods as research has proven it to be beneficial for short term and long term health benefits.

Meditate dear, just meditate

Most of you may not have the luxury to stretch out completely in your workspace that is why techniques like mantra meditation or *pratyaahaar* come in handy. These can be done in the sitting position without making any sound or requiring any major space.

Again, a specific regular time has to be given to train your mind to shut out all activity and switch off for 10 minutes. This can be done by simple counting; breathe in for three counts, hold for four counts and breathe out for as long as you can.

Keep up the smile

I know you must have heard this a million times, but still there is no better remedy for life's problems but to smile through it all. It has been scientifically proven that smiling releases serotonin in the body which helps in regulating appetite and thirst, and even mood swings. It can help reduce ageing by loosening up the tired facial muscles. It helps in healing. And yes, of course, it works great for personal charm, helps maintaining relationships better and it's contagious in a good way.

Teamwork

There is a saying that if two people sing together with different tunes and continue singing like that, they will eventually pick up notes from each other and as a result sing an altogether different tune which will be harmonious than the previous one. This applies not just to the process of singing but life as well. In our workplaces also you are bound to pick up things from people surrounding you, even the negativities, so pick your team wisely. If you are lucky enough to get the choice, otherwise learn to keep yourself in good company and never run away from discussions. It is said that even the carefully hidden facts come out very easily during discussions. The story of Chinese whispers has its origin in Veda, that if in a circle of people, one person starts a message and passes it on to the other the result in the end may be completely different from what it had started from. The reason this is relevant here is that sometimes taking up information beyond what you can hear or see is very important. People who have been the most successful have relied on a great sense of intuition that they have kindled for many years. Say yes to an opportunity with a pure heart; it will never go waste.

Management

Just like energies of the universe, the skills of management at workplace also have a dual nature, both feminine and masculine. In other words, some matters at the workplace may require a soft approach and some may need a hard approach. Of the various aspects of management, feminine skills work better for negotiation, bargaining, training, persistence, patience and perseverance which require flexibility, poise, intuition, compassion and emotion. So in areas where in these skills are required, females tend to outperform their male counterparts. In the Vedas, 'stree' does not always refer to the female gender; it signifies female-like quality, or in other words, emotive or flowing energy. What defines whether you are a male or a female is just a sign or an organ, also the origin of the word 'lingaa'. This does not mean your mind will exhibit the same qualities as your lingaa. We all have both masculine and feminine aspects to our personality. So it has been seen that some skills, generally identified with female, work spectacularly well in the field of people management, human resource, the service sector, training and even core selling. On the other hand, in a world which is dominated by men, masculine traits can take one a long way into the corporate journey. The masculine qualities mentioned in Ayurveda are courage, strength, assertiveness, aggression, ambition, competition and leadership. So masculine traits are best used to develop strategy, skill development, analytics, logistics, recruitment, risk management and core administration.

So, therefore, one should be flexible in using these traits as and when the situation requires, one is not complete without the other. You cannot survive with only a certain set of skills, belonging to only one group.

Health policy

My advice to all corporate firms working in India, whether of indigenous or international origin, is to take into account the lifestyles of the locals while creating and maintaining a health policy. The health of any company is defined by the health of its workforce. Unfortunately, for us most of the multinationals here follow the system originated in the country of their origin, American and German firms will generally have American and German policy, food menu and nutritional aspects. Just as local language is important for marketing to make a connect, the knowledge of local life is important for employee management. In most of companies there is a fixed menu, overlooking the current nutritional status of the employee, no attention is paid to seasonal variations or climatic influence or the freshness of sourced vegetables, even frozen vegetables are also used. Food menu should be region and climate specific. The principles of Ayurveda need to be integrated with the current corporate health plans for a better, effective and healthier employee management. Guidelines may be western, but implementation has to be Indian. Here are some steps that can be followed:

- The menu in all organizations should include herbal teas along with regular offering of tea and coffee, as they are easily available and are cheaper alternative to aerated/energy drinks in India.
- Employees must get 10 minutes of break especially in the evening for meditation or a power nap or stretching, which

may be optional but taking a break should be compulsory during the day.
- Most of the companies are doing their bit in their own way by conducting regular tests. It is of dual help as it keeps the employees' health under check and gives the company an idea of the health of its work force. A recent development in one of the Asian countries was to increase taxes on food containing saturated fats simultaneously reducing taxes on essential food items. For example, obesity in India is a major health issue and this step could be implemented here. Health check done by labs is very mechanical as it may tell you about a chemical imbalance; however, it is very difficult to assess the SQ or Stress Quotient through these tests.
- Stress can be assessed through nadipariksha, as there is no instrument to measure pain because it is a feeling, so is stress. Pain, same as stress, suggests that there is an ongoing imbalance in the body. Also, there is no instrument to measure stress. Blood pressure is a manifestation of stress, it can be measured. Manifestations or diseases take years to develop and before taking their full form disorders or stress keep accumulating in the body. In an adverse case scenario, this accumulated stress may abruptly show up as an acute and a critical condition as. A health check-up which is comprehensive in terms of quantitative and qualitative aspects of human body and mind is the need of the hour.

Statistics speak

Statistics show an increase in corporate death due to stress has increased by twofolds in the last two years. This issue alarming and needs to be addressed in a systematic way immediately.

Choices

Any person in the society is served with multiple choices in the daily life. The working mother is forever pressed for choices between spending time at work and with family. There are a lot of questions that I am asked by working professionals, common ones being: what to eat at office parties or what to do with changing shifts. I suggest, at office parties always eat something fresh like a salad first because it will help refresh your taste buds and the mind; also it is a healthier option to start with.

Hiring

If you nurture the seed itself, the fruit is going to show sooner or later. For a new employee, along with the induction session, the HR department should lay emphasis on lifestyle and dietary training. This is fairly important because there are a lot of changes that occur from an academic life to a corporate life, so from an active lifestyle, sitting time will increase, so at least a heads-up is required. At the end of the day, the hired resource is the company's asset, his/her health will add to the productivity in the long run.

Leadership

Though every employee is an equal and important contributor, it is imperative for the senior leadership, who are the people with strategic roles who looking after not just themselves but also the organizations, to lead a healthier lifestyle. One error or a bad decision can cost a large number of people. If these people lead the way and strictly follow Ayurveda, the effect will be visible in just a couple of months.

Women, Ayurveda and gender equality vis-à-vis health

With the increasing awareness about gender equality, or the lack of it, it is becoming easily clear that women do have to work twice as hard to earn the same pay in most industries. Also, the competition would not pay heed to whether you are a mother or not, or whether you are pregnant or dealing with post-partum depression. These are practicalities of life that consume time, energy and health and may end costing you in monetary terms also. Women's need for fitness is twice as more as compared to men, as performance also continues after eight hours of job, which includes taking care of family, cooking, etc.

In India this is a harsh reality that husbands of working women spend the least amount of time in doing domestic work compared to men from other parts of the world. Please understand that in the top leadership positions all around India women form only 1-2 per cent of the numbers. The bodies of Indian females put up fat more easily as it has been programmed that way, so if an Ayurvedic lifestyle is followed by working women, it will help them in not only keeping their weight in check but also prepare herself for a long and fruitful work life for years to go. This book has alternatives to the western way of living and eating which, if applied to everyday life, may prove beneficial for Indians. I urge every working mother to follow these as much as they can, since it is always good to see a fit working mother with a great job and healthy kids and who is applauded for her work outside as well as inside home.

> *The reason for all inability is fear; do not fear anything and you will be able to do anything.*
> —Charak Samhita

Chapter Five

Ayurveda for Students

Learning is a lifelong process, and we, as students, learn at every step. Vedic sciences have described the qualities of a student in various instances, an ideal student should be first and foremost fit physically, disciplined, eager, virtuous, obedient towards the teacher and willing to follow orders and not be not afraid to ask questions which are relevant.

Indians boast of a 'guru-shishya parampara' which has existed for handreds of years. In this system knowledge as well reasonable skills were handed over from an expert teacher to a worthy student. This tradition was the target point of many invaders and foreign rulers, what happened as a result was that the system of education has been completely westernized. The principle of Vedic sciences encourages the student to learn new sciences as well. However, the method to instill various kinds of knowledge has to be skill-based and should be used in practical ways on a daily basis.

However, the modern concept of education is very different and it requires a more doctrine approach. Most of what is taught in high schools may not come to practical use. It is quite theoretical. Barring some, most of the wisdom and education are learnt at home through parents only. So, therefore, parents are the first and the most important teachers in a student's life. You can make small changes in your life to see their wonderful reflection in your children, which will help them in school and later in life as well.

Therefore this chapter is for all the urban parents who have far less time to give to their kids than their parents had. Here is a quick reckoning guide to review what you may already be doing and some additions from a doctor's side to keep your child healthy and happy. Remember the student/child has a keen eye for observation he/she will follow whatever you do.

Lead and feed by example

Let's start with focusing on eating. Kids will want to eat what you are eating from a very young age but all these habits should be inculcated methodically, when one becomes a parent one has to raise the standard of nutrition in life, failing in which will result in nutritional disorders from an early age which are the most common these days. Nutritional disorders are not passed onto children by genes; these are habits which a child picks up eventually. Once, one of my patients had asked me to prepare medicine for her child. The child could eat two burgers in a flash but failed to finish even one home-cooked meal in the whole day. The child was not a stubborn one, in fact, when asked about it gently, my patient explained how junk food was perceived as a perk in her house and it was indeed her husband who had made the concept of junk food so alluring that she gets rewarded for every good deed with a pizza or a burger and so on and so forth. So, home-cooked food has become sort of a punishment, which is sadly a routine in many urban homes. A child with a sick stomach will hardly be able to focus on studies or even daily routine. A child is a commitment to the divinity of life, one needs to be in tune with the goodness of life to do justice to such kind of commitment.

Solution

Herbal drink made by adding cinnamon and honey to milk might become a family craze if the father/mother drinks it every day. A sense of excitement has to be created over home-made food. This should act as a reminder to follow the daily and seasonal routine mentioned in the previous chapters to set an example in eyes of children.

Monitor

The daily sugar intake of children per day must be watched as too much sugar may produce increased hyperactivity in younger children which hinders their learning process, in teenagers it will eventually lead to weight gain, obesity and other complications. Sugar intake includes white flour, candies, chocolates, cold drinks, sweets, tea/coffee, etc.

Avoid

Tea/coffee drinking should be by choice and the later you indulge the better it is for your body. I have seen many parents suggesting tea/coffee as a home remedy for cold/cough. This is to state clearly that caffeine is in no way therapeutic for cold or cough; in fact it may aggravate the symptoms because of its drying nature, dehydrating quality. The initial soothing effect is because of the hot water that is actually making the beverage. Tulsi, ginger or liquorice tea, etc. have proves to be efficient remedies for these seasonal allergies.

All work and no play

The ill-effects of sitting for more than eight hours per day are quite conspicuous for corporate job holders, which for them is binding and compulsory. However, the current generation of children is sitting for more than eight hours a day from a very early age, so lifestyle disorders are on the rise. Juvenile diabetes is becoming common day by day. Incidence of high cholesterol i.e. hyperlipidaemia can be seen in the age of eight and even six years. The government here is doing a lot by including yoga in the curriculum especially in state-run boards. However, the addition of sports in curriculum or basic mandatory sport training is also suggested for most public schools. Most urban parents prefer sending their kids to air-conditioned schools; this is also a standard-defining point in school comparison for parents. Air-conditioned air is basically recycled air of the same premise lacking in moisture, continuous exposure to such environment can cause respiratory allergies, skin dryness and lethargy. It reduces prana level in the body, which results in the basic lack of initiation and enthusiasm. To add to this the fierce competition, momentary success and general unsatisfaction in our world has created a void in the lives of our children which becomes the parent's job to fill or remove. Life has become all about virtual success on video games or popularity on social networking websites, none of them, sadly, require physical exercise.

Solution

Start/continue spending time with your kids while walking or doing physical work yourself. Playing physical competitive sports at home with parents instils a lot of confidence in children.

Monitor

Check frozen and fried food intake as they are high calorie food items plus they create a lot of ama (metabolic toxins). The symptoms of accumulated ama in the body are as lethargy, decreased immunity and low stamina. Consumption of such products creates a vicious cycle of temptation towards a particular brand, etc.

Include

Ghee/olive oil make for a good choice as dressing on food for your kids, these help in decreasing the glycaemic index of foods plus are good neuro-muscular tonics, will keep cravings for high calorie sweet foods at bay, a child should have at least five small meals throughout the day to keep the blood glucose at uniform levels, this will also reduce levels of crankiness and irritability. For students, it will serve as memory booster.

Daily stretches

For teenagers and young adults who are studying throughout the day during competitive and board examination, a 20-minute session of relaxing the body is a must. It has been actively researched that studying with adequate sleeping and resting has gotten better results due to enhanced retention of knowledge and improved cognitive function. On the contrary, studying continuously for more than 10 hours without taking any break to sleep/exercise would result in inadequate retention of knowledge.

Sitting for long can produce pain or lethargy in the body; stretches are needed to pull the body out of this stress, especially in case of teenagers who sit for long durations. Instead, children must indulge in some light stretches to relax their bodies.

For example, start by doing stretches for toes by bending and relaxing them, rotate the ankle joint clockwise and anti-clockwise seven times. Next, sit in padmasana or lotus posture or cross-legged posture, take five deep breaths and do stretches for shoulder by flexing the forearm when the tips of fingers touch the respective shoulders and make a big zero in the air by rotating the shoulder, kids carry a lot of stress in their shoulders, and usually have a hunched back and this will help to maintain a good posture.

Technology: A boon or a bane

The plethora of audio–video content being bombarded in various ways is dangerous especially for students. Manufacturers of leading touch interface products suggest avoiding giving tablets and mobile to children. They repeatedly issue a warning, as research says it is known to cause a variety of psychological disorders, for example increased incidence of ADHD (Attention Deficit Hyperactivity Syndrome) in children using tablets for more than two hours per day consecutively for a year. In this syndrome, there is decreased concentration and reduced attention span leading to loss of memory in kids, another aspect being increased incidence of social isolation on the pretext of lack of confidence and common sense. The second significant problem is excessive use of search engines for studying and completing school projects. Whatever information is available free on the Internet is either sponsored or marketed.

Solution

Reading together is a fun activity. Stories like *Panchatantra*, or folklore provide quintessential basic solutions to everyday problems. The children of today's generation are lacking in the earthiness and in some cases even common sense. Parents, as providers, have to understand that child may not value simple things in life if he/she is given everything very easily. The usage of phones or tablets begins due the glamour attached to it.

Monitor

Electronic usage in children must be limited. For example, taking printouts from the Internet will seem like a viable solution; however, it is strictly discouraged in countries where search engines have originated. Charts, handmade drawings not only work on reflexes but also help in increasing creativity.

Good habits

A habit of newspaper/magazine reading must be instilled. For younger children, it is good to look at pictures or identify letters, for older children newspapers help them keep abreast with current happenings around them.

Travel

Travelling and exploring, help in enhancing our five senses. As adults, we slowly become so certain of ourselves and the knowledge we have attained that sometimes the little things a child knows might seem unimportant. However, answering the questions of the child will enhance the intelligence of the parents first, followed by the child.

Activities that enhance brain function

Music

Music, especially playing any instrument, rejuvenates almost all of the neural synapses of the brain and the mind feels relaxed. It is a sort of meditation. In some schools, instrumental music is part of the curriculum as well.

Sleep

For performing well in analytical and mathematical examinations, one has to sleep for more than eight hours, as in these subjects knowledge acquired over a period of time comes to use only after sleep. In subjects like literature and social sciences sleeping for six hours helps recollecting everything learnt.

Children who are light sleepers are likely to have lower memory retention than deep sleepers, do not scold the child on being a deep sleeper or wetting the bed, etc.

Activity

Fun extracurricular activities make the brain sharper. It is said that the best way to bathe is to take a bath like an elephant does. Elephants are known to have a very strong memory. Even routine work when done in a fun way becomes relaxing for the brain.

Listen

The best way to learn from others and gain knowledge simultaneously is by listening. A good listener is always a good speaker.

Discuss and debate

The best ideas and sharpening of brain occur via discussion. With the continuous hustle and bustle of office, discussions and debates at home tend to decrease with the increasing age of children.

Herbal home remedies

Herbs like brahmi, shankhpushpi, ashwagandha, guduchi, etc. are excellent neuro tonics, they can be given on a daily basis to children. These have been used traditionally for hundreds of years and are readily available.

The psychology of fear

Children, like adults, also suffer from phobias. Everything may seem fine with your child but he/she might be suffering from an exam phobia or peer performance pressure. In today's ever-changing world a person with a unique skill set is earning much more than a good academician. A skill or an art only has led to the immense technological advancements. Many examples of great inventors come to our mind that were average or below average academically but have done very well for themselves later in life. Do not scold your child unnecessarily, and, most importantly, don't make rules you yourself do not follow.

Observe

Observe your child for any unexpected behaviour or habit. Remember, you are being observed as well, even more minutely, and with great expectations.

There are four ways for the one who wants to attain knowledge: from the teacher, from his fellows or colleagues, from his own intelligence (self) and from the natural cycle of time and the experience that grows with time.

Chapter Six

Ayurvedic Cooking

Mother Nature has created every shape, colour and flavour possible. One might argue that many foods that are available nowadays are man-made; however, just as we may create a variety of chocolates from the simple cocoa beans, the flavour of simple chocolate is really tough to beat. Our creativity can only be healthy when it is in accordance with how nature makes food for us. We need to imitate nature in many ways to produce the desired nutritious and wholesome output. There can be hundreds and thousands of recipes, however, sometimes humans tend to overcomplicate things. There are lot of delicacies in the name of food that are disappointing in terms of nutrition to the body. If you offer overly cooked food to animals like a dog or a cow, they will refuse to eat. If the life of any food particle is lost by excessive food processing and preservation, animals will intelligently refuse it even if they are kept hungry for a long time. This is a basic survival instinct, unnatural food effects the body in so many ways it is tough to enlist it in one go, the damage can be slow and vicious in nature. The current increase in the number of lifestyle disorders is a reflection of the ignorance of a whole generation. The decrease in the mortality has not provided subsequent betterment in the quality of day-to-day health or efficiency or intelligence. The traditional culture of food running since the advent of civilizations still, by far, provides the best nourishment to the human body, in comparison to the modern advancement in food science which is, in my view, lagging far behind.

Does food have life? Indeed it does, this is called the 'prana' of food. Grains have a longer shelf life than fruits; cooked grains, however, have the same shelf life as a fruit because cooking makes the carbohydrates simpler to get evaded by bacteria. Also stale, overcooked, undercooked food has lower pranic energy. Canned and microwaved food has a languid feel to it, cooking is one basic survival skill, I believe, everyone should know. Even if one doesn't cook on a regular basis, just understanding the basic process will help gain knowledge of the art and science of food. Being closer to nature by sorting, cutting, peeling the natural outputs like vegetables or fruits or grains one ends up understanding and admiring the beauty of God's creation and the effort put into that process of honouring natural produce makes us so grateful. With numerous years of technological evolution can we even remotely create a pattern as intricate as on a mint leaf packed with so much flavour, aroma and therapeutic qualities? After spending time with some farmer's family it made me realize how much effort is put into obtaining one grain of rice. Two days later, while at a wedding, I was deeply saddened to see heaps and heaps of the same grain being wasted. Ayurveda has time and again said that *adharma* continuously done by a society on the whole is the reason for natural calamity or *janpadudvansa*. Considering the plight of farmers in India on one hand and the sheer wastage of resources on the other, aren't we inviting the wrath of nature? The beloved monsoon which makes India so unique is diminishing day by day due to the over exploitation and wastage of all the available resources. This way we all are contributing to adharma. Let us pledge to not waste even a single grain because anna or grain is brahma (food is divine). Food has lost its importance in the modern world, the reason why junk food has become sort of a priority in a weekly diet is quite a strange phenomenon. Many people claim they diet to detoxify the body. But they are actually cheating their bodies just for a little while and thereafter craving junk food. The tongue is a very tricky sensory organ of the body, for the five seconds that the tongue makes the decision of eating a certain food, our consciousness loses its ability to reason that a certain food may be harmful for us even if it tastes good. Also, cravings for certain foods signify emotional disturbances. By satisfying the tongue, one may forget whatever topic is bothering but that is again for just three to five seconds; the mind can only be distracted by food, it will never be satisfied with it. So eat via the process of intelligence and selection and not any distraction. Anything (be it tea/coffee) that you cannot do without is a hindrance to your path of evolution in life. Continue to experiment with your palate. This chapter shall provide some basic techniques of Vedic cooking with different recipes which will simply make it healthy than your regular way of cooking.

The process of digestion as it is said in the Vedic texts starts with either the sight or smell of the food. We might not be able to tell the difference between a piece of a mango or a banana if the sense of smell is not present and eyes are closed. So the enjoyment and nourishment of food is part of the process of fulfilment of the need of all aspects of the physical body. Food is best eaten with hands as the nerve endings of the fingers also get stimulated, the temperature also gets checked and the texture of food is also enjoyed. Ayurveda says that in a day the body needs different textures (how the food feels to the tongue) to satisfy the sensory organs. Ayurveda describes four kinds of food textures to achieve satisfaction while eating—lehya (to be sucked by the tongue), peya (for sipping), bhojya (for chewing simply) and bhakshya (crunch or extraction by using the teeth).

Maharishi Charaka had said our body is a result of eating food, so is also the disease caused by food. The wholesome diet is pleasure (health) and unwholesome diet is pain (disease). A person who eats wholesome diet does not require medicinal treatment and no medicine will completely cure a person who does not eat wholesome diet. Medicine will provide you with treatment and the right diet vis-à-vis any treatment will lay solid grounds for complete recovery and rejuvenation of the body. The modern aspect of nutrition lays emphasis on the quantitative parts of food with the division based on the difference between carbohydrates, proteins, minerals and vitamins. The concept of diet management relies on the requirement of calories per day and diseases arise with the increase or decrease in the intake which leads to positive or negative calorie balance. Ayurveda, on the other hand, places emphasis on the nature of food, the taste it contains, the method of preparation, their emotional effect, food combinations and incompatibility, quantity, place and time of intake, individual capacity (agni) and constitution (prakriti). Therefore, Ayurveda has a more wholesome holistic qualitative approach more than just a quantitative one.

Ayurveda has laid extra emphasis on the exact identification of taste. It says that there are six basic tastes:

- Madhur or sweet
- Lavan or salty
- Amla or sour
- Katu or pungent
- Tikta or bitter
- Kashyam or astringent

The sixth taste is an addition in comparison to other modules; Ayurveda says that astringent foods also have an after taste.

Whatever we eat is called *ahara*. This ahara is changed into 'ahara-rasa' or in a form that can be assimilated by the body. This ahara-rasa is further absorbed in form of 'saar bhaag' (what it is important for the body) and thrown out of the body in the form of 'kitta bhaga' (the part from which waste i.e. sweat, urine and faeces is produced). Many a times I see in patients that even though the cyclic expulsions of kitta bhaag i.e. sweat, urine and faeces are present the formation of sara bhaag is not accurate. As there is absence of any major problem, no attention is given to the digestive system. However, this (saar bhaag) forms the basis of formation of all the bodily tissues and the *ojas*. If the saar (food essence) is not qualitatively normal, what happens in these cases is that there is formation of ama. Ama is a special concept of Ayurveda which lays importance on the finer aspects of digestion. This is how we explain that despite of a rich diet, many people tend to suffer from vitamin deficiencies. When there is formation of ama and the saar bhaag or the important nutrient part of the food is not processed correctly. It may be inadequate as in case of deficiencies or excessive as in case of obesity.

Virudhdhahaar

All food articles possess their own rasa (taste), guna (characteristics), virya (potency) and vipaka (post-digestion effect). Some food stuffs also possess prabhava, an unexplained effect. The fate of food articles within our body depends on the state of our digestive fire. When two or more food articles having different taste, energy and post-digestion effect are combined, the digestive fire can become overloaded, inhibiting the enzyme system and result in the production of toxins.

Poor combination of food items can produce indigestion, fermentation, putrefaction and gas formation and, if prolonged, lead to toxaemia and diseases. For example, eating bananas with milk can diminish digestive fire, change the intestinal flora, produce toxins and cause sinus, congestion, cold, cough and allergies. Although both of these foods have a sweet taste, a cooling energy, their post-digestion effect is very different—bananas are sour while milk is sweet; this cause confusion in our system and results in toxins, allergies and other imbalances.

Some of the incompatible food items are:

Food item	Not to be consumed with
Beans	• Fruits, cheese, eggs, fish, milk, meat, curd
Eggs	• Fruits especially melons, beans, cheese, fish, milk, meat, curd
Fruits	• As a rule shouldn't be taken along milk, curd
Grains	• Fruits, tapioca
Honey	• With equal amount of ghee by weight • Honey should not be consumed with hot liquid. Or, heated up or taken with any hot/boiling liquid. Honey with hot water in the morning does not lead to weight loss
Hot drinks	• Mangoes, cheese, fish, meat, starch, curd
Lemon	• Milk, curd
Melon	• Everything, especially dairy products, eggs, fried food, grains, starch • Melons more than other fruits should be eaten alone
Milk	• Bananas, cherries, melons, sour fruits, bread containing yeast, fish, meat, curd
Nightshades e.g. potato, tomato	• Melon, cucumber, dairy products
Radish	• Bananas, raisins, milk
Tapioca	• Fruits, especially banana and mango, beans, raisins, jaggery
Curd	• Fruits, cheese, eggs, fish, hot drinks, meat, milk, nightshades • Curd should never be cooked with other food items and should not be consumed at night, and should not be taken during rainy and spring season • Curd should be taken with honey, soup of green beans, ghee or amla powder

This is a very short list. To determine which combinations are incompatible there are some rules that one must follow:

- In cold areas and during cold season, food articles which are cool in potency and unctuous in character are generally wrong food combination for that area.
- Likewise in warm areas and during hot season the food articles with warm potency and pungent or bitter taste should be avoided.
- Taking a heavy meal when one is having little appetite (agni/fire).
- When one is habitual of taking dry, unctuous, warm food articles then the food articles with cold potency and unctuous in character prove to incompatible food combinations.
- Food articles with warm potency mixed with food articles with cold potency.
- Eating anything while holding any of the natural urge like urine/stools.
- Milk with sour fruit or salt.
- Food articles which are either overcooked or undercooked or stored for long after cooking.
- Eating anything without one's willingness.

Cuicina Ayurvedica

Those of you who are reading this chapter will surely be interested in cooking and some of you may have straightaway jumped to this section to see which recipes have been included here. Most of you know recipes of some kind and may expect some boring recipes like daliya, etc. Yes, daliya is an excellent and healthy food item but it would be boring to eat it every day. I understand that eating is one of foremost pleasure in life, therefore, I lay a lot of emphasis on the healthy exchange of exciting flavours. Vedic cooking's principle is the right technology for food; it is said that everything we eat is part of universal intelligence, cooking of combining these to enhance human intelligence so that they do not hamper your health at all.

We heal and nourish our body everyday with food. This is our process of taking in energy in form of solid matter. We are what we eat, what we eat defines how our daily, weekly or yearly life might shape up. No matter how time-pressed you are, make sure one meal of your day is hearty and with family or in someone's company you enjoy, as eating well is a celebration in itself. It is a reason to celebrate life every day. Cooking should be a celebration too as that way only we can enjoy our food. I believe that one doesn't cook with ingredients, one cooks with emotions (*bhavas*). One of the gastrointestinal disorders mentioned in Ayurveda is caused due to the ill wishing of the person cooking the food. Also it's always advised to take out a portion of your food for someone other than your kin so that the divine is also happy. Vedic cooking is about awakening the spirit of Annapurna within you and transferring that piece of your beautiful energy via food to other human beings.

How a person cooks tells you a lot about the state of mind of that person. If you give a vegetable to a person to dice, notice it and you will know how he is at work. A chef does it finely, swiftly and perfectly. A mother of three little kids might do it so hurriedly that it may be uneven, but will be thoroughly checked. A patient cook will treat it gently and cut it evenly and check for any shortcomings. The third category of people are the passionate home chefs who will benefit most from this content. Cooking is giving a part of your energy via food. A good meal is not which is served steaming hot or icy cold, or which is spicy or sweet. A good meal is that which is purely satisfying. The current state of most Indian urban kitchens is in midst of confused and fast-paced transition. Even school lunch box these days are packed with junk food. So this is a small but a strong attempt to break the vicious circle of tasty recipes based on all-purpose flour i.e. maida or potato or 'bhoona masala' mix.

Grains

Humans are meant to eat a variety of grains. On the contrary, what has happened is due to a number of agricultural revolutions that have occurred over a period of years, the growth of rice and wheat has become economically most yielding for the farmer. Therefore, the biodiversity of nature has been transformed into commercial fields of wheat and paddy. A grain which is very common may not be the best in terms of nutrition to the body. For example, corn which is the most extensively grown crop in the world has the highest glycaemic index of all grains i.e. it takes the least time to transform into glucose after digestion. Moreover, it absorbs a lot of fat while cooking, therefore loads up the body with extra amount of fat. Rice and wheat are a bit better, since a lot of wholewheat products are actually quite good for the body but how much wheat you can eat? Our tongue craves for different kinds of food, especially for vegetarians eating only a two-grain diet may simply lead to vitamin deficiencies. As most of the grains that are available easily in the market like corn, rice and wheat have only a certain group of essential amino acids required for the body. So diversifying our grain palette which not only leads to a variety of taste, but only a multigrain diet can provide wholesomeness. I get a lot of queries if rice should be consumed daily. More than 60 varieties of rice have been described in Ayurveda in addition to those; there are various hybrid varieties that have come up. So to label rice as good or bad is quite an unscientific generalization; the indigenous population of rural India has been eating rice for centuries and are completely fit. The problem is with the refining process; the basmati rice which is available over the counter is a refined version of the traditional rice. This process increases the glycaemic index, decreases the fibre and vitamin content of rice. The variety of rice which is eaten in the villages is not as smooth and bright as the refined rice; therefore it is not much appreciated in the cities because of lack of aesthetic appeal. Similarly, the refining of wheat turns it into maida which is also called all-purpose flour. Maida is fattening because of the very high glycaemic index and almost no fibre content. Our taste buds have gotten used to the extracted sweetness of basmati rice and maida. Most of the fancy eating is based around the consumption of these only. On the other hand, the humble, poor man's grains like millet, etc. are sidelined, waiting for their turn to be in the spotlight with recipes centered around them. India happens to be the world's largest producer of millets but urban households sparingly use any of them. A number of patients especially kids are suffering from gluten intolerance or celiac disease these days. This means they tend to suffer from gastronomic symptoms if they eat wheat as it has protein called gluten, so not only for that member but grain-base of the whole family changes which has better effects on not only the suffering individual but also on the general health of the family.

Let me highlight some of the brilliant grains that nature has provided us.

Barley

Barley contains eight essential amino acids plus additional fibre and vitamins in comparison to the staple wheat. Also barley has been an integral part of international cuisines as well as the traditional Indian ones, not only can it be made into a khichdi or a roti, it can be made into a cool and cleansing summer salad, recipe of which has been included here. Whole grain flour of oats (jai), used to make Indian bread known as *jarobra* in Himachal Pradesh, is just an example of how we tend to overlook gems like oats which are very much a part of our heritage. The commercialization of oat and oat bran has led to its addition to biscuits and hence naming it as digestive. The dietary fibre provided by grains is the micro-fibre and hence cleanses the little pores of the body.

Millets

Millets is the collective name given to a lot of grains. Unlike rice and wheat that require many inputs in terms of soil fertility and water, millets grow well in dry regions as rain-fed crops. By eating millets, and other grains we will be encouraging farmers in dry land areas to grow crops that are best suited for those regions. This can also serve as a step towards sustainable cropping practices where by introducing diversity in our diets, we respect the biodiversity in nature rather than forcefully changing cropping patterns to grow wheat and rice everywhere.

Millets are one of the oldest foods known to humans and possibly the first cereal grain to be used for domestic purposes. They have a good shelf life too; they can be stored easily for two or more years without any deterioration. They are highly nutritious, non-glutinous and non-acid forming foods. Hence they are soothing and easy to digest and can be used as a staple for the gluten-intolerant. They are considered to be the least allergenic and most digestible grains available. Compared to rice, especially polished rice, millets release lesser percentage of glucose and over a longer period of time. This lowers the risk of diabetes. Millets are particularly high in minerals like iron, magnesium, phosphorous and potassium. Finger millet (ragi) is the richest in calcium content, about 10 times that of rice or wheat. Ragi is very popular in southern parts of India; it is made into porridge, uttapam (salty pancake) and milk malts. If it is eaten for breakfast, it keeps the body cool, retains energy for a long period of time. Some of the common variety of millets are Barnyard Millet (jhangora), Finger Millet (mandua/ragi), Foxtail Millet (kangni), Kodo Millet (kodra), Little Millet (kutki), Pearl Millet (bajra,), Proso Millet (barri/cheena) and Sorghum (jowar).

Also, internationally alternative to staple grains such as quinoa and amaranth are quite in vogue and served as starred dishes. Some of you may have heard about the saag of cholai along with the dal i.e. the seeds eaten as a staple dish in western Uttar Pradesh and Bihar. Amaranth is nothing but cholai seeds used extensively in desserts especially in the USA. When you get to explore the food heritage of India, one finds so many hidden treasures. The navratras that come twice a year is about being grateful to the staple grains, and replacing them with pseudo-grains which is tapioca (sabudana), amaranth (ramdana), shingada (water chestnut) and kuttu (rhubarb). Out of these the flour of water chestnut is the most wholesome and sabudana the least nutritive. One more interesting thing that I would like to share here is that the famous Japanese buckwheat noodles are also made from kuttu atta by a hand technique. So if you want to make an interesting dish in the Navratras, you can serve buckwheat noodles with a vegetable stew. These fasts are given a more ritualistic angle to get good complacency with the scientific technique of fasting. One should, at least, have 30 days a year which are grain-free i.e. exclude staples and have a more inclusive diet. The fruit of Barnyard Millet, mentioned in the list of millets, is, in fact, saama chawal used as an alternative to rice; it is gluten-free and can serve as a good alternative to rice in case of diabetics. It is easily available in the common market. Barley stew is a traditional method to break the holy fast of Ramzan in the Saudi Arab, so some traditions are worth keeping and they are here for a reason.

Here are a few recipes packed with nutrition to help you stay healthy.

BARLEY SUMMER SALAD

Cooking time: barley—30 min and salad mixing—10 min

Ingredients:
½ cup barley, cooked till soft
½ cup mixed peppers
¼ cup cucumber
2 stalks of celery
8-10 cherry tomatoes
Home-made vinaigrette with lemons, olive oil, black pepper, chilli flakes, black salt

Method:
Mix all the vegetables to the barley once it has cooled down and toss in vinaigrette. Mix well.

This is best eaten at room temperature.

JOWAR CHOCOLATE CAKE

Cooking time—40 min

Ingredients:
1 cup jowar flour
1 cup chocolate powder
1 cup yoghurt
2 tbsp oil
¾ cup sugar

2 medium cucumbers, grated
1 tsp baking soda
1 tsp baking powder

Method:

Mix together oil, yoghurt and sugar. Then add the grated cucumber. Keep aside. Sieve flour, chocolate powder, baking powder and baking soda together. Gently fold them into the mix. Grease a baking tray and pour the batter into it. Bake it in a preheated oven at 220 degree Celsius for about 40 minutes.

Using cucumber may sound a bit weird, but believe me it's very important to use something as watery as this, because jowar flour tends to make the cake dry. It is this cucumber that would make it moist. And the cake does not taste of cucumber.

~

KHICHDI

Cooking time—30 min to 45 min, depending upon the grain

Ingredients:

Can be made with either 1 cup jowar/barley/daliya
1 cup moong dal
Salt, to taste
Turmeric
Ghee
1 tsp cumin seeds
Few potatoes, diced

Method:

Soak the grain overnight. Cook grain till soft. Add moong dal, diced potatoes, salt, turmeric and pressure cook for another 2 whistles. Heat ghee in a pan and add jeera to it. Let the jeera splutter. Add it to the jowar khichdi. Serve it hot with papad, curd, ghee and pickle.

AMARANTH CHIKKI

Cooking time—30 min

Ingredients:
1 cup gur
3 spoons brown sugar
1 cup amaranth
Ghee, for greasing the plate

Method:
Heat gur and brown sugar in a pan together to get a 'chashni' of the consistency that can form beads when you put it in water. Add popped amaranth to it and switch off the gas. Use a greased plate to put this mixture and roll it off into a thick chikki, then cut into pieces and let it cool.

PONGALI

Cooking time—45 min

Ingredients:
Can be made with either ½ cup cheena/ragi
1½ tbsp jaggery
3-4 cups water
⅔ cup moong dal, cooked
2 spoons ghee
Cashew and almonds, roasted
2-3 cloves
Cinnamon powder

Method:
Cook cheena millet in water until soft. Drain excess water, if any. Add jaggery,

some cloves and some cinnamon. Cook for 3–4 minutes. Add about 2 karchis (⅔ cup) of cooked moong dal. Cook for another 2–3 minutes. Heat 2 spoons of ghee and roasted cashews, almonds and any other nuts of your choice. Add it to the cheena. Serve hot.

~

KONJI
Cooking time—45 min

Ingredients:
Can be made with ½ cup cheena/barley/jowar
3-4 cups water
1-2 onions, diced and sautéed
1 green chilli, sliced
¼ cup curd, whisked
Spices—coriander, salt, pepper powder (according to taste)
Few drops lime juice
½ tsp mustard oil

Method:
Boil cheena in water. Cook for about 10 minutes, until soft. Drain excess water, if any. Let it cool. Add diced and sautéed onions (without oil), sliced green chillies, coriander, salt, pepper powder and whisked curd. Serve with a dash of lime juice and mustard oil.

~

TABBOULEH
A Lebanese dish (sometimes the name of the dish makes a big difference), Tabbouleh is simply broken wheat mixed with colourful veggies. In Arabic countries it is served with egg or non-vegetarian food items. Vegetarians can substitute that with fresh paneer or cottage cheese by added it in the end. The grand old healthy daliya can be made interesting in this way.

Cooking time—45 min

Ingredients:

1 cup wholewheat or jau dailya, dry
1 cup water
1 cup mixed vegetables (onion/carrots/cabbage/spring onions/corn kernels/ bell peppers/zucchini/peas/broccoli/beans)
Salt and pepper, according to taste
25 gm paneer/boiled egg
Coriander for dressing
1 tsp oil (mustard/sesame for sautéing vegetables)

Method:

In a heavy-base pan roast daliya till brown, add water when aroma comes. Simmer till water reduces. Set aside.

In a separate pan add oil, vegetables from thicker to thin i.e. add carrot and beans first then bell peppers and softer one like zucchini and broccoli in the end. Add salt, sauté till they soften. Now add the cooked daliya mix thoroughly. Add paneer/boiled egg. Garnish with black pepper and coriander leaves.

Serve hot or with curd.

Cooking with yoghurt

I am asked the maximum questions regarding yoghurt or dahi. It is a product of fermentation so, therefore, contrary to popular notion, it is not cooling in nature, it is vidahi i.e. it increases heat element in the body. It should be absolutely avoided during any kind of fever. Also it is Stroto avrodhak, i.e. it blocks the channels in the body, so it acts as a medicine during diarrhoea, watery stools, irritable bowel syndrome, etc. It is famous because it contains healthy bacteria for the body. However, by adding herbs to it, it makes for a healthy snack and serves as a tonic for the gut. After blending it becomes a smooth drink, therefore called a smoothie and many people are selling the same in name of health drinks. Here are some smoothie suggestions.

VATA SMOOTHIE

Preparation time—5 min

Ingredients:
A pinch of hing (asafoetida)
3 gm roasted cumin or bhoona jeera
Black salt (according to taste)
0.5 gm saunth or dry ginger
1 cup yoghurt
1 cup water

Method:
Mix all the ingredients using a blender to create a smooth consistency, which will pacify vata dosha, especially gaseous distension of the body. You can also add fresh mint or coriander leaves and pepper powder to this smoothie.

PITTA SMOOTHIE

Preparation time—5 min

Ingredients:
1 cup yoghurt
1 cup water
4 gm dried mint leaves
5-10 fresh coriander leaves
8-10 fennel seeds (optional)
Black salt, according to taste

Method:
Mix all the ingredients with yoghurt and water to make a pitta pacifying smoothie, ideal for summers. You can also add rose water and honey to make this smoothie

sweet. Alternatively, you could add amla powder with honey.

KAPHA SMOOTHIE

Preparation time—5 min

A pinch of asafoetida (hing)
⅛ tsp dry ginger (saunth)
¼ tsp black pepper, black salt, according to taste
1 cup yoghurt
1 cup water

Method:

Use a blender to mix all the ingredients with yoghurt and water to make a kapha pacifying smoothie. Diabetics can use roasted cumin, methi seeds and black pepper powder to control their sugar levels.

BAKED VEGETABLE SALAD

Baking is a method of slow cooking; hence it is advocated by Ayurveda. In the absence of modern oven, food was covered and sealed off in earthen pots to be cooked off in heap of husk and cow dung for hours, thus creating a mini oven. It makes food more delicious as all the juices are kept intact. Also, Ayurveda suggests consuming vegetables by cooking them.

Cooking time—20 min

Method:

Bake vegetables in oven for 160 degree Celsius for 15-20 minutes with seasonal veggies. Garnish with salt, pepper and home-made dressing and enjoy this hot.

SOUPS

Yusha or soup occupies a very special place in Ayurvedic cooking. Yusha ignites digestive fire, detoxifies the body and many herb infusions bring in that extra flavour. *Charak Samhita* contains numerous recipes of medicinal soups for these purposes.

In the modern Indian kitchen, however, soups have taken a packaged or Chinese form. A soup with high amount of ajinomoto or monosodium glutamate (MSG) will damage the liver than cleanse it. Following are some soups that you must try at home.

~

PUMPKIN SOUP

Cooking time—30 min

Method:

Boil and mash 500 gm of pumpkin. Add some water and check consistency. Season it with black pepper and rock salt. Roast kalonji seeds in a pan to be added as a garnish. You can also add coriander or parsley leaves and black cumin seeds to enhance its flavour.

~

SPINACH SOUP

This brightly coloured vegetable makes for a great soup; addition of moong dal helps takes away the strong pungent taste.

Cooking time—30 min

Method:

Boil 500 gm spinach and 2 tbsp of moong dal; adjust quantity of water and grind in a blender/mixer. Add roasted black cumin seeds/sesame seeds as garnish.

~

VEGETABLE STEW/MINESTRONE/MIX VEG SOUP
Cooking time—20 min

Method:
A recipe used all around the world with various seasonal additions and subtractions, this is a great dinner recipe for everyone. Cut vegetables of your choice and add water. Add and bring to a boil then mash or semi-mash and garnish with fresh coriander leaves or herbs.

~

Healthy snacking

How many times should one eat? The three-meal theory has been disregarded by dieticians who believe that small, regular meals throughout the day do the magic. The meals have to be placed carefully, though, so as to have a wholesome effect without the heaviness. You can prepare a whole lot of munchies at home, here are some suggestions.

MAKHANA MURMURE
Cooking time—15 min

Ingredients:
100 gm makhana
50 gm almonds
50 gm murmure
2-3 green chillies, finely chopped (optional)
25 gm groundnuts (optional)
Salt, according to taste
Black pepper, according to taste
4-5 dhaniya seeds

50 gm chiwda (optional)
½ tsp ghee

Method:

In a pan, heat ghee, add green chillies, makhane, almonds, murmure and roast for some time, stir regularly to avoid burning, and optional ingredients can be added at this stage. Roast these ingredients as well. Let it cool down.

Store this in a glass jar to have it at any time of the day.

~

AAM PANNA

Cooking time—60 min

Ingredients:

4-5 raw green mangoes
Water
Spices—roasted cumin powder, black salt, roasted fenugreek seeds

Method:

This is a great cooling drink for summers. Boil the mangoes with four times the water to soften it. Let it cool and then remove the peel, mash the pulp with a blender, add spices like roasted cumin powder, black salt and roasted fenugreek or methi seeds, it has a protective action against heatstroke and is a great tonic for digestion.

~

JALJEERA

Preparation time—30 min and presentation time—2 min

Method:

The commercially available ones are laden with excessive salt. Strictly avoid them. At home, mix roasted cumin powder, dried mango powder, dried mint powder, black salt, and store in a jar. Soak tamarind overnight, remove seeds and blend it. Add the dry ingredients to make a great appetizer for all seasons.

~

RASAM

This traditional south Indian preparation is surely not to be missed for a variety of reasons.

Cooking time—30 min

Ingredients:

2-3 tsp ghee
2 tsp tur or urad dal
1-2 red chillies, dried
3-4 peppercorns
3-4 cloves garlic
2-3 tomatoes
½ tsp turmeric powder
Salt, according to taste
Water
Coriander leaves, for masala and garnish
500 ml tamarind juice
Some cumin seeds

For tempering:

1 tsp mustard seeds
1-2 red chilli
1 tsp cumin seeds

Method:

Heat a wok with a teaspoon of ghee. Fry tur or urad dal, peppercorns and red chillies till the dal becomes brown. Then add the garlic pearls and some pieces of tomatoes and sauté for 10 seconds and switch off the gas. Now add the cumin seeds and well-washed coriander leaves with the roasted mixture and grind to coarse paste and keep aside. You can add water, if necessary, while grinding.

Heat a pan with extracted tamarind juice. Add turmeric powder, salt and remaining tomatoes. Add half teaspoon of sugar. Let it boil till the raw smell of tamarind goes. Now add the grounded masala to it. Wait till the bubbles start forming. Mix well. Switch off the gas.

For tempering, put mustard seeds, red chilli and cumin seeds in a teaspoon of ghee. Garnish with coriander leaves.

VEDIC MILK

The best possible substitute for milk malts is by mixing dry fruits like walnut, almond, melon seeds and pistachio (unsalted). Add raisins, some saffron and store in a jar. Herbs like turmeric or mulethi (liquorice) powder can also be added. Chopped dates can also act as a blending agent. Add to milk and boil together to blend in the flavours. By adding pure vanilla essence, kids will find it tasty.

A strong digestive fire is a symbol of good health, when one gets good ingredients to make food, when one has methods to cook good food and when good food satisfies the agni, these are the fruits borne out of good karma. To maintain the good karma, one should be grateful and compassionate and distribute to others what one is getting.

Chapter Seven

The Way to a Healthy Life

Water is an inevitable aspect of Ayurveda. It carries certain energy within itself; this is one of the basic reasons to explain this change in the environment of different regions. Water is much more than H_2O. You might have read that the water of holy springs helps in removing ailments entirely. What is life without belief? Vedas suggest that it is the intention of the person serving water to you that actually enters your body when you drink it. Our cooking is mostly water based and even our body is 70 per cent water. So the intent of the cook will definitely have an effect on the dish. Ayurveda also mentions that the reason of ill-intentioned cooking as one of the causes for gastrointestinal disorders (one more reason to eat home-cooked food). What your mother cooks has a distinctive feeling of satisfaction and fullness irrespective whether you remember the taste or not. The Indian royals, years ago, employed 'maharaj' (cook) who used to regularly meditate to be able to cook for them. Happy chefs have successful restaurants. Fast-food chains have a mechanized dullness to it which is different from the nutrient issue. So you may end up eating more and more to fully satisfy yourself, which, I think, is the main cause of obesity. I believe it is not the obesity that causes depression but vice versa.

Coming back to the humble granny, who gives a note of caution every now and then, was rooted scientifically. Their generation had a fewer diseases because these little details mattered a lot back then. What is required is the balance between the old and the new. The usable water quantity per Indian is decreasing considerably. It is a renewable resource, but taken for granted.

There is no set daily quantity of how much water one should drink, but a minimum of four-five glasses is required but if one feels thirsty more than twice a day means that you are already a bit dehydrated and should increase your water intake.

Water taken on empty stomach calms the body, soothes the mind and detoxifies the internal system of the body. Water should not be taken just before a meal as it dilutes the digestive fire and also water taken just after meals slows down digestion and might lead to weight gain and health loss. So the right way would be to take small sips of water throughout the day to ensure proper hydration and digestion.

In case of any stomach disorders, one must drink water boiled with a bit of cumin seeds or hot water specially boiled for 20 minutes taken throughout the day in sips is the most wonderful remedy for any health disorder.

Indian spices

Years ago, India was called the golden bird (in Hindi, *'sone ki chidiya'*) amongst Europeans. Apart from the amount of wealth, the abundance of spices produced here was also a contributing factor. Indian spices contain abundant medicinal properties which, if used in the right way, can bring down the medical bill quite a lot.

Maharishi Charaka says that the point of origin of disease will also have the remedy. Say, if a disease has originated in South Africa, the local herbs may provide the best solution. *Suranjan* (colichium indicum) has traditionally been used as a herb for the treatment of gouty arthritis, and even colichine, which is used for the treatment for the same problem, is an extract from the same herb.

What I again want to assert here is that since spices are indigenous to the soil of India, the ailments which have originated here can be easily prevented and cured by scientifically proven antidotes like black pepper, turmeric, cinnamon, cardamom, asafoetida (hing), coriander, basil (our very own tulsi) to name a few.

Similarly, fennel (known as saunf locally) is part of Italian cuisine as well; here we use only the seeds. On the other hand, potato and tomato are not indigenous to India. However, Indian cooking contains the maximum potato dish. Indeed, the effect of foreign invasions is reflected on our food culture which from simple, fresh and spiritual process turned into a contest between mismatched flavours. Coincidentally, marigold, which is of beautiful saffron colour and is so hugely adorned on idols of gods and goddesses, is again not of an Indian origin.

In Sanskrit we say '*anna is brahma*', food is God itself, and food is the universe itself. So whatever is offered to God should be consumable, should be taken afterwards, here is where the concept of *prasadam* originated. So that faith and offerings to the holy do not end up in waste and are consumed afterwards. Rose petals, coconut, oil, panchamrutam all have significant healing properties but au contraire marigold (flower) does not. Thus generates awful amount of waste which pollutes the environment which is antagonist to the purpose of puja that is to purify the environment.

Pickles

Ayurveda is a very humble science, it tells us to embrace new norms in a healthy way and to constantly experiment with age-old traditions in accordance with the requirement of the present age. One of the very prominent traditions in India is of pickling food. These originated when there was no protection against food shortage that may occur due to a natural calamity (if any). These were methods of food preservation for a longer period of time, so in a way pickles are one of the foundation stones of the present day food packaging industry.

Ayurveda suggests eating pickles and fermented foods in strict moderation as condiments. Here, a pickle refers to preservatives of vegetables and fruits without oil and balanced with spice. The sour taste in this pickle sparks the agni (digestive fire), enhances appetite and promotes digestion. It's better to include these healthy condiments during winter season as the spices used have a warming effect on the body. Beneficial for pacifying vata, but pitta and kapha prakriti people need to exercise caution as pickles eaten in large quantities aggravate pitta dosha in the stomach and the salty liquid nature of the pickle increases kapha.

The tradition of home-made pickles has dwindled and nowadays one sources the pickles from the market in a plastic oil-filled jar. You will be shocked to know how much preservative and salt goes in your body daily without even consuming any pickle because of the packed food (namkeen, etc.) items included in our general diet. And in the case of addition of salt-laden, oil-encumbered, spiced fruit i.e. pickle the liver has to work to metabolize that and the kidney has to work to flush out unwanted ions through our urine. Always remember that the mere release of stool is not the prerequisite for health. The proper digestion, absorption of macro and micro nutrients is required.

Excess salt and preservative is a deterrent to the optimal functioning of metabolism. Bread, milk, paneer, juices generally, come in packages at our homes. They contain preservatives and are considered safe. Then add to it packed snacks like chips, namkeen, etc. which are like salt weapons, even packed chutneys and pickles. You might add or deduct according to your diet but one cannot avoid preservatives in essentials like milk, but you can avoid namkeen (salty snacks) and market-sourced pickles. Patients even argue with me that not all recipes of pickles are bad but I want to strictly caution you against the oiled ones. Oiled varieties contain a lot of allergens and toxins which are like poison to anyone suffering from skin disorders, hyperlipidaemia and heart diseases. This was a requirement before the green revolution had not hit us, but not anymore.

Excess salt causes water retention in the body and has been linked as a precursor to diseases like hypertension (high blood pressure) and metabolic disorders like thyroid dysfunction. It is one of the major causes of early whitening of hair and excessive hair loss. I feel that the whole of this generation has lesser hair compared to previous generation because of the excess intake of salt and refined flour.

Vegetarian vs non-vegetarian

There is a perpetual question that patients ask me, and that is my opinion on non-vegetarian food. The answer is a situational one. Firstly, eating non-vegetarian food or being a vegetarian is not an issue of morals or religion that is advertised to be. It is not just a matter of choice; it is also, again, a matter of region and situation. Man started as a gatherer and hunter so we have been eating non-vegetarian food before even the appearance of civilization. Secondly, with the advent of agriculture there are so many varieties of food substances available that being a vegetarian logically becomes the preferable choice as human intestines are indeed longer than natural carnivores so food stays inside us for a longer time. Thirdly, non-vegetarian food takes a longer time to digest and indeed creates a lot of ama (undigested metabolites in the body). Ama can be related to imperfect metabolites and oxidative stress. In addition to this, people who do not do strenuous workout will surely develop a disease of metabolism if they remain habitual carnivores.

In the 21st century India, there is abundance of unaware vegetarians who will argue that it is fine to consume alcohol (especially beer) and cheese because they are both vegetarian foods. Now, fried potato with beer or fried chicken with beer are going to show on your belly no matter what option you prefer. Which is more harmful is a tricky question. Vegetarianism has become a reassurance that nothing will happen to your gut and you can eat whatever with whatever tastes good. Taste lasts for five seconds on your tongue; health is something one has to live with throughout his/her life. All unhealthy combinations are eaten up in the name of taste e.g. fried items with alcohol. There is ample amount of description on various types of alcohol; it is used as a medicine if it is product of natural products like flowers, fruits and herbs. Synthetic alcohol is compared to 'visha'. It increases the absorption and cycles of metabolism and then depresses it. There have been numerous researches on the benefits of red wine which can be co-related with *draakaasav* which is an Ayurvedic recipe of preparing controlled fermented grape juice with dhatki flower (woodfordia fructosa). It is advised to take draakasav in case of a disorder of immunity or in months of extreme cold. So in a cold climate, with excessive physical labour, non-vegetarian food becomes a valid choice. In a tropical country with the usual jobs, vegetarianism is the essential choice. For a patient suffering from tuberculosis, which occurs from kshaya (malnutrition), it is said to give *'mansa rasa'* or non-veg soup even if it has to be given against the will or knowledge of the patient. But anyone who has a sitting job will have to follow simple vegetarianism, sooner or later, by choice or compulsion.

Therefore, any region where tropical conditions are prevalent, a rice-based vegetarian diet is best suited and in cold climate non-vegetarian food will work if preferred by will and choice.

Positive thinking

The purpose of life on the Earth is to evolve. It is the only constant principle in natural life. However, evolution has optimized our brains for survival; it has not necessarily brought happiness. Research suggests that the brain is very good at building brain bitten (neural matter) from negative experiences. We learn immediately from pain or a negative experience, you know 'once bitten, twice shy'. As our ancestors evolved, they needed to pass on their genes. And day-to-day threats like predators or natural hazards had more urgency and impact on survival. On the other hand, positive experiences like food, comfort of home, mating is good, but if you fail to have one of those good experiences today, as an animal you would have a chance at one tomorrow. But the human brain is relatively poor at turning positive experiences into emotional learning or neural structure. Positive thinking by definition is conceptual and generally verbal and most conceptual or verbal material do not have a lot of impact on how we actually feel or function over the course of the day. A lot of people have this kind of positive and look-at-the-bright-side kind of attitude, but deep down they are very frightened, angry, sad and disappointed. Any faith that has arisen from a negative impact on the brain is bound to last longer, but will not be fruitful and progressive for you.

The solution lies in training your mind to turning the present moment of your life into a profound experience of positivity which would eventually alter your neural structure (brain matter) to make you a happier human, in a way one can completely change their thought process with disciplined happier thoughts. Our mind has many thoughts, the thought of continuously talking to ourselves again and again and going through the course of day, juggling work, personal life. It tends to become this washing machine just whirl pooling, making sound and going round and round until a moment of epiphany comes that we are stuck in life. This is called a 'vritti', to stop all the vritti (circular thoughts) you simply need to embark upon a realization journey and prioritize your duties accordingly. The problem here is that everybody says that they are fine and have gotten used to this compromise termed as routine life. As important it is to take care of the body, it is equally important to take care of the mind because it is unbounded, never-ending, most exciting resource of our life. I will describe a few simple techniques of training the mind which have been clinically proven and I often suggest these to my patients who have shown considerable positive results. These are easy to do and can be done anywhere in any comfortable position.

Meditation should not be used as a pill for relieving stress, it is like crash-dieting only to lose weight and not maintain a healthy lifestyle, and to see the weight coming back in most cases. This comeback weight is even more difficult to lose. So you need to get yourself out of this pill-popping culture. Meditation is the best preventive solution to handle any problem, to confront all the emotions in the right way without getting distracted and losing the whole point of life. A study by Harvard University suggests that an average mind spends about 47 per cent of time in wasteful thoughts and some more hours for sleeping. Considering we are only here for 100 years, which is a very small time compared to the age of the universe, we are spending half of the time in sleeping and half in distraction, where is the time to actually live?

Just imagine yourself standing in a busy, noisy and crowded vegetable market bustling with energy, sounds of the vendors, aromas of the fruits, and colours of the veggies in the midst of all this you cannot lose the focus on the calculation of the price so that you can pay exactly what you are supposed to. If you lose focus then somebody might take away your bag. Similarly, in life you have to mind your business; talk, listen, communicate, observe, pay your dues, comeback and enjoy your time. In all this, do not get attached to anything because you are here for a purpose, you have to do your karma and get going. If you get stuck or fall or cry, nobody will care anyway. Everyone is there to do their own business.

Meditation is not about stopping your thoughts; it is about witnessing the moment without getting attached to it. In meditation do not control your mind, do not contemplate, there is no need to concentrate, but just rejuvenate. One has to experience anxiety, pain, joy, peace and satisfaction all in one go while becoming thoughtless and mindful. Don't push too hard, just pursue the following techniques and find your very own rhythm in your time. Just remember to do it twice every day for 15 minutes without any distraction for an experience that is profound and majestic.

Sit in a comfortable position with adequate back support, first close your eyes and check your breath, make it slower. With each inward stroke notice how the air is filling up in your throat and chest. Relax and breathe out. Breathe in by using your abdominal muscles slowly, count (in your mind) if you require and breathe out.

Technique

- Start with five counts in and six counts out, this is one round; do 10-15 rounds in a minute. Depending upon your capacity, this should be the start to the required 15 minutes. You can repeat this cycle for four to five minutes, if you lose count in the middle; don't fret because that is the objective anyway to lose count and knowing your breath.
- Next exercise is about forceful rhythmic expiration and deep inspiration; this has to be more strenuous than the previous one as you have to use all the respiratory muscles, both the primary and the accessory ones. The rhythm should be increased from one breath cycle lasting for five seconds to one breath cycle lasting for four seconds then to one breath cycle lasting for three seconds and then for two seconds. This decreasing indent has to be repeated four-five times in one session. When you do this you will breathe better and all the stagnated 'mala' (mucous) will come out. You might sweat or may lose the rhythm of count but that is entirely OK, it is just breathing. You have been doing it from the very first moment of your life; it will be the last thing at the end of life. It is the sign that you are alive. So by being aware of your own breath you will eventually become more and more aware of life.
- Next technique is to see the happenings within the mind, when you are in the process of doing the above two, there might come moments when you are blank. Thoughts will come and go, let them be, don't pay attention, take your attention back to your breath and to yourself. These 15 minutes you ought to be not enslaved by your commitments, not ashamed by

your mistakes and not happy about your success. You are just with your breath.
- The fourth technique is just about repeating a hymn in the mind; this may be a word of two or two and a half akshara. For example with 'h' and 'ma'. Start with an inward breath with the first syllable (h) and exhale with the second syllable (ma), make it slow or make it fast, depending on your rhythm. When thoughts come into your mind, keep them aside, come back to the initial syllable, if you lose the syllable come back to it anytime you want, you may change it, increase the length or decrease it. Whatever it may be, it is your canvas, paint it. Spend seven to nine minutes within this canvas.
- The fifth and final technique is Om chanting. This can be done at home or at a peaceful place. Breathe in deeply and breathe out saying 'a–o–m', the 'a' and 'o' part should be shorter and the 'mm' part should be stretched while chanting. You can create a sound as this is not in your mind; it is like after going deep in to the ocean you try to resurface. Repeat this five to eight times. You will get to see the effects within two to three days and if you do this right, you will never stop meditating.

Water is life, the ultimate elixir, the medium for all beings to survive. It is the most available, irreplaceable, natural drink for enlivening the prana i.e. energy of life.

Fall in Love with Yourself Again!

Life is full of limitless possibilities, but to enjoy that the mind has to be clutter-free only then can we make most of innumerable opportunities that might knock our door. Reinforcing negative thoughts will not help you in any way. In fact, reinforcing positivity may help create the space in your mind that can be used to store good memories and thoughts. The universe's work will get done anyway; whether you are game enough to do it will ascertain what you end up doing after all. It is a wonderful life, you see; God, as a life-giver, would like you to just live it. If you spend too much time in telling how good He is or saying how your version of Him is better, you will lose the whole objective of supreme power. It's like when you are in love with someone and you spend too much time describing their beauty to others rather than being with him/her. By adopting healthy Ayurveda habits you can lead a happy life now and always!

Acknowledgements

One can never express enough gratitude towards the divine; however, one should never miss an opportunity.

I am grateful to Ayurveda, which completely changed my perspective towards life. The idea of this book came from the moment I fell in love with this wonderful science. I was inherently a city girl but felt that there was a missing link between the urban and the traditional system of medicine. From then I have been working towards this goal of making people aware of their roots.

I would like to take this opportunity to thank:

My patients, whom I met in the course of my practice and who are all unique and have contributed to the examples given in the book.

Reeta Malhotra, my mother, who has been a pillar of strength for me and has helped me through all my difficult moments in life.

Dharini Bhaskar, who first spotted my blog and initiated me into writing a whole manuscript on Ayurveda.

My editor, Sunayna Saraswat, for her dedication and commendable inputs.

And my husband, Nippun, for his continuous encouragement as it would not have been possible to write or complete this book without his contribution.